Innovation and Export

Smart Innovation Set

coordinated by
Dimitri Uzunidis

Volume 37

Innovation and Export

The Joint Challenge of the Small Company

Manon Enjolras

iSTE

WILEY

First published 2021 in Great Britain and the United States by ISTE Ltd and John Wiley & Sons, Inc.

ISTE Ltd
27-37 St George's Road
London SW19 4EU
UK

www.iste.co.uk

John Wiley & Sons, Inc.
111 River Street
Hoboken, NJ 07030
USA

www.wiley.com

Library of Congress Control Number: 2021945495

British Library Cataloguing-in-Publication Data
A CIP record for this book is available from the British Library
ISBN 978-1-78630-620-3

MIX
Paper from responsible sources
FSC® C013604

Contents

Acknowledgments

This book is drawn from the work of a French doctoral thesis on the topic "Methodology for analyzing the innovation and export capabilities of manufacturing and process SMEs: identification and characterization of a common space with a view to developing a multi-criteria decision support tool", conducted between 2013 and 2016 at the ERPI laboratory of the University of Lorraine (located in France). They were financially supported by the UIMM, the F2I, the Lorraine regional council as part of the PRINCIP research chair as well as the InnovENT-E initiative of excellence (IDEFI). This thesis has paved the way for new research projects that also feed this book. They have themselves benefited from the support of the CNRS and the University of Lorraine (PEPS Mirabelle CIIPME project), as well as the Lorraine University of Excellence Initiative of the PIA2 from the French government (ANR-15-IDEX-04-LUE).

First of all, I would like to thank the Research Network on Innovation (RNI), as well as the ISTE Group, for giving me the opportunity to publish this book by awarding me the Honoris Causa prize for the promotion of research in the study of innovation. It is a real pride to see our thesis work valued in this way and a great opportunity to continue to develop it within a long-term research project.

I would also like to thank the ERPI laboratory of the University of Lorraine for allowing me to carry out this thesis and for allowing me to build my research path on a daily basis within its team. I would also like to express my gratitude to my two thesis directors, Mauricio Camargo and Christophe Schmitt, without whom none of this would have been possible.

I would like to thank all the practitioners and institutions that agreed to participate, in one way or another, in this work and to devote some of their precious time to it. Thanks to the different laboratories that have been kind enough to welcome me during these last years, allowing me to give an international dimension to this research work: INRPME Trois Rivières, HEG Fribourg, the Industrial Engineering Department of the USACH, the University of San Juan and the National University of Cuyo.

Finally, I would like to warmly thank my family and friends who have always supported me in my projects, both professional and personal.

Introduction

Innovation and internationalization have been identified as two of the main driving forces of economic growth (Pla-Barber and Alegre 2007; Bołkunow 2019). And while globalization has changed the competitive playing field for all companies, this is especially true for small organizations within which available resources are limited (Etemad 2004; Szczepanski 2016).

The internationalization of a company can take several forms: import, external growth, direct/indirect export, etc. For this research work, we focus on a specific mode of internationalization: exporting. Several studies point out that exporting is one of the most common ways to enter the foreign market in the early stages of SME internationalization (Bianchi and Wickramasekera 2016). Thus, throughout this book, we will define exporting as the internationalization strategy aimed at positioning our products and services outside the geographic boundaries of our home country.

Exporting provides an additional source of demand via a larger market or by enabling the creation of a new market (Monreal-Pérez *et al.* 2012). In addition, international competitiveness helps boost the domestic market and pushes other companies to internationalize (DiPietro and Anoruo 2006). However, international markets are characterized by much stronger competitive pressure than domestic markets (López *et al.* 2005). SMEs are thus generally hampered by their difficulties in mobilizing the strategic resources needed to enter and succeed in international markets (Etemad 2004). However, if we look at the main figures on the competitiveness of companies, and more particularly small companies, it appears that despite the difficulties they face, SMEs do export. However, although SMEs employ a large share of the workforce, they are under-represented in global trade relative to their contribution to national economies (OECD 2018), particularly in the industrial sector. Direct exports by SMEs account for only 3% of the total SME manufacturing sales, compared to 14% for large companies (WTO 2016). In contrast, the rate of export participation appears to be clearly correlated with company size. The participation of medium-sized companies[1] (59%) is higher than that of micro or small companies[2] (9% and 38%) and is quite similar to that of large companies (66%) (WTO in English 2016). Thus, it seems necessary to strengthen export support, particularly for smaller structures by helping them better mobilize and optimize their strategic resources.

On the other hand, innovation has always been synonymous with success for companies, but it was generally considered a privilege reserved for some, mainly the large high-tech multinationals. However, the rapid industrial evolution linked to globalization has led all companies to constantly renew themselves in order to more quickly react to the changing conditions they face: shorter product life cycles, changing customer requirements, an evolving technological environment, aggressive competition and environmental regulations, among others. As a result, SMEs, perhaps even more than other companies, are also affected by these challenges. They are therefore forced to integrate innovation[3] into their survival strategy. Nevertheless, managing innovation for small businesses in traditional sectors remains a difficult task. Although an SME is generally considered to be an environment conducive to innovation, it is not always successful (BPI France 2011b). Their flexibility seems to be a major asset, but their lack of access to resources and skills can prove to be a major constraint (Szczepanski 2016). Innovation represents a risk for SMEs, and they are not always able to assume it (European Commission, 2016b). Thus, innovation

1 As defined by the OECD TEC (Trade by Enterprise Characteristics) database: microenterprises: <10 employees; small enterprises: 10–49 employees; medium enterprises: 50–249 employees; large enterprises: >250 employees.

2 The gap between micro and small enterprises is explained by the fact that the majority of microenterprises are not export-oriented, due to their specific activities (local services, for example).

3 In this book, we use the definition of innovation supported by ISO 56002 (2019): a new or changed product, service, process, business model or organization.

is clearly identified as a success factor for SMEs, but the difficulties they face hinder the proper management of their internal processes.

Supporting SMEs in their innovation and export activities is, therefore, a major challenge. Indeed, SMEs are the most common form of business organization and the largest provider of employment in the world. Indeed, they represent more than 95% of industrial enterprises in OECD countries (European Commission, 2016a). Consequently, they represent an extremely important economic stake and supporting them in their innovation and export efforts is therefore crucial. It seems essential to help them improve their internal practices in order to change their behavior and improve their performance while adapting to the environment in which they operate.

In this respect, there is currently a real political and economic will to take into account the considerable stakes involved in the development of SMEs. All over the world, numerous support services are offered, at the regional or national level, by public and private institutions. However, and despite the important commitment of the European Union and local authorities (innovation and export have been identified as priorities for action at the European level, such as the Horizon 2020 program), support for SMEs in innovation and international activities is not always adapted.

For example, it seems that current support services are mainly represented by financial or informational incentives (Enjolras *et al.* 2015). If the main difficulties encountered by SMEs, both for innovation and export, do indeed concern access to resources, it is nevertheless worth questioning the relevance of a temporary increase in resources without the organization and strategy necessary for their proper exploitation being put in place. In the case of incentive schemes, the resources provided to SMEs are mostly *ad hoc*, without the organizational and strategic difficulties associated with innovation and export being really addressed. Several European Commission reports have emphasized that the most effective type of support seems to be individualized support, as it allows direct action on the internal organization of SMEs by improving their skills and strengthening their resources (Francis and Collins-Dodd 2004). By building skills and changing the routine practices and activities of SMEs, the proposed support appears to be more sustainable and effective (European Commission, 2016b). Thus, it would seem that sustainable and targeted support for SMEs is about empowering them with strategic, comprehensive, and cross-cutting skills and resources.

On the other hand, although the Interreg 2014–2020 strategy devotes an entire axis to increasing the cross-border competitiveness of SMEs and 8 billion euros to SMEs, the support initiatives for SMEs tend to adopt a compartmentalized vision of the aid they offer. Support for innovation and export appear to be two disconnected initiatives, whereas a trend towards coupling these types of support is gradually emerging, according to the European Commission (2007). Indeed, recent studies have shown that companies that are able to manage innovation and international activities are simultaneously more profitable and sustainable over time (Love and Roper 2015).

According to BPI France (2011a), more than one innovative SME in two is present on the international market. This observation highlights the existence of a link between innovation and exporting, and innovation clearly appears to be a driver of international activities. SMEs that innovate are indeed more likely to engage in global markets than non-innovating companies. Process and organizational innovation, for example, can increase company productivity by reducing production costs and enabling SMEs to achieve the minimum level of efficiency required to cover fixed export costs. Through product innovation, marketing innovation and innovative branding strategies, SMEs differentiate their products from those of their competitors, allowing them to gain market share in international markets (OECD 2018). In particular, greater flexibility and a strong ability to customize and differentiate products can give SMEs a competitive advantage in global markets over larger companies, as they are able to quickly respond to changing market conditions and increasingly shorter product life cycles. For example, a report on the behavior of European SMEs (FedEx 2015) shows that fast-growing SMEs are almost twice as likely to export as declining or stagnant SMEs. Indeed, some inter-country niche markets are dominated by SMEs, and small innovative companies often become key partners for large multinationals to develop new products or serve new markets (OECD 2018).

From a theoretical perspective, the study of the link between innovation and export in the context of SMEs represents a very important research topic in the current scientific literature (Love and Roper 2015). Specifically, much work focuses on the direction of causality regarding the impact of one on the other. This paradigm is supported by two theories: self-selection (Monreal-Pérez *et al.* 2012; Boso *et al.* 2013; Raymond and St-Pierre 2013) and learning-by-exporting (Kafouros *et al.* 2008; Golovko and Valentini 2014). Self-selection considers that innovation positively impacts exporting.

It is considered a necessary condition for exporting, allowing a company to be sufficiently armed to access international markets. Learning-by-exporting, on the other hand, considers that it is international experiences that promote innovation within companies through the acquisition of technical, commercial, and/or cultural knowledge that enables them to envisage the development of innovations. Whether it is self-selection or learning-by-exporting, these two theories consider the link between innovation and export through a causal relationship. They are interested in the impact of one activity on the other and reason in terms of cause and effect. These two theories coexist in the scientific literature and are regularly tested through numerous empirical studies. However, the results greatly diverge from one study to the next, and it is impossible to validate or invalidate either theory from a general perspective (Enjolras *et al.* 2016).

The study of the link between innovation and export, when studied in terms of causality, thus leads to a controversial debate for which it seems difficult to find a consensus. This is why some studies try to go beyond this causal vision by proposing a vision in terms of complementarities. Innovation and export would not only be activities that have an impact on each other. They would be complementary activities: if we engage in one, it facilitates engagement in the other (Golovko and Valentini 2011). This notion of complementarity also seems to have an impact at the institutional level. There is currently an emerging trend to couple innovation and export support schemes (European Commission 2007), but this is a topic that is very little addressed in the literature. It would seem, therefore, that the study of innovation and export in SMEs requires a different perspective, one that aims to consider them jointly rather than through a cause-and-effect relationship.

By way of summary, given the context of innovation and export in SMEs, three observations can be made:

– the first concerns the limited performance of SMEs on international markets and their difficulty in setting up a successful innovation process. This can be explained by a preponderant constraint directly linked to their small size: the lack of resources and the difficulty to put in place the right conditions to exploit them. Thus, SMEs wishing to progress must structure their internal processes, prioritize their actions and identify adequate improvement levers in view of the means they can mobilize;

– the second observation concerns the incentive nature of the support offered to SMEs. The schemes mostly offer financial support or information, which appears to be one-off assistance rather than real long-term support. It, therefore, seems necessary to offer support based on individual advice, allowing the company's organization to be modified by changing the practices and activities in place, and thus offering more sustainable support;

– the third observation concerns the link between innovation and export. In the scientific literature, this link has traditionally been considered in the form of a cause-and-effect relationship. However, a paradigm shift seems to be emerging, highlighting the need to propose an approach that breaks with this causal vision in order to take into account the complementarity that exists between innovation and export. It is a question of considering these two activities together and not in terms of the impact of one on the other.

Thus, through this research work, we propose considering the relationship between innovation and export from an original angle. The objective is to formalize the innovation–export relationship in SMEs through the complexity paradigm (Morin 1977). This formalization leads to the identification and characterization of a common conceptual space between innovation and export capabilities. This common space gathers the joint innovation–export activities that an SME must develop in order to simultaneously progress in terms of innovation and export. It, therefore, represents a priority area for action to be promoted among companies in order to encourage them to modify their internal practices to exploit synergies and thus optimize the mobilization of their resources. From an operational point of view, the valorization of this common space requires the proposal of a support tool to evaluate the degree of mastery of the companies concerning the practices, resources and competencies that make up this common space. The first objective of this diagnostic tool is to draw up a profile of the companies evaluated in order to identify the activities they need to develop as a priority in order to successfully complete their export and/or innovation process. The second objective is to propose personalized recommendations based on their strategy to promote the emergence of innovation–export synergies. The implementation of these recommendations allows the company to progress both in terms of innovation and export, relying on synergies to mobilize its resources in an adequate and optimized way.

The ambition of this book is, therefore, to support a joint and complex vision of innovation and export in SMEs and to apply it to the problem of the business world. Initiated in 2013, through a thesis (Enjolras 2016), the work carried out is part of the PRINCIP research chair (research cluster on innovation and SMEs' innovation capability) at the University of Lorraine and was conducted in collaboration with the IDEFI InnovENT-E project (initiative of excellence in innovative training). This research work is also a multidisciplinary initiative between industrial engineering and management sciences, promoting the need for an alliance between the creation of representation frameworks to share vision and meaning (scientific approach specific to management sciences, based on value creation and a cognitive approach to individuals and situations) and access to modeling formalisms from complex systems (a scientific approach specific to engineering sciences that favors instrumental development). Thus, this work exploits the strength of this multidisciplinarity combined with a strong field vision provided by numerous partners from the regional SME ecosystem. They have indeed several academic, industrial and institutional forms of support (UIMM[4], F2I[5], CNRS University of Lorraine[6], Lorraine University of Excellence initiative of the PIA2[7], Lorraine Regional Council, etc.). This book presents the results of this work in order to promote a joint vision of innovation and export, as well as the exploitation of the resulting synergies among both SMEs and institutional support actors. Through the design of a multi-criteria decision support tool aimed at highlighting these synergies, this work proposes a concrete application of this joint vision and its contributions, particularly in terms of resource optimization, which is a particularly crucial issue for SMEs.

The book is composed of five chapters divided into two complementary parts. The first part exposes and justifies the scientific positioning of the research. It, therefore, approaches the problem of innovation and export in SMEs from a theoretical point of view. Chapter 1 aims to introduce and relate the main concepts mobilized in order to arrive at a robust theoretical

4 *Union des industries et métiers de la métallurgie,* French Union of Metallurgical Industries and Trades.

5 *Fond pour l'innovation dans l'industrie,* Fund for innovation in industry.

6 Primary Support Exploratory Projects (*Projets exploratoires premier soutien*, PEPS) to foster interdisciplinary exploratory research.

7 *Plan d'investissement d'avenir 2 de l'ANR Lorraine université d'excellence*, reference ANR-15-IDEX-04-LUE.

framework. This chapter thus proposes an original vision of the innovation–export relationship by applying the complexity paradigm. The main result of this chapter is the identification of a common innovation–export space at the origin of synergies. Chapter 2 aims to define and characterize the common innovation–export space through the identification of joint activities. It, therefore, presents the process of identifying activities specific to innovation and those specific to export before describing the identification and characterization of joint innovation–export activities that enable SMEs to simultaneously improve their ability to innovate and export.

The second part adopts a more operational stance by seeking to transform the theoretical common space into a repository of joint practices at the origin of a functional decision support tool. The aim is to exploit the conceptual results of Part 1 to give them substance through the development of an evaluation tool (Chapter 3), and then applied through six case studies (Chapter 4). The tool, called "PE2I" (Potential Export and Innovation Index), was thus designed and tested with six French SMEs, from manufacturing or process sectors, of different sizes and technological intensity. This section provides feedback on the evaluation tool, its implementation and the performance of its results in order to identify prospects for improvement (Chapter 5).

PART 1

The Relationship between Innovation and Export in SMEs

1

The Innovation–Export Relationship: A Complex Vision

The relationship between innovation and export is the subject of particular attention, both in the professional and academic worlds. Several studies have shown that innovative companies are also those most present internationally, and vice versa. However, the support systems dedicated to these activities tend to offer differentiated support, exclusively oriented towards either innovation or export. Moreover, within the companies and organizations themselves, the people in charge of one or the other activity are different. Thus, from an operational point of view, the vision of innovation and export remains relatively compartmentalized, although there is a tendency to combine support systems dedicated both to innovation and export. These trends are linked to the theories mainly developed in the scientific literature adopting a causalist vision of the innovation–export relationship. However, this causal vision is sometimes challenged by empirical studies in favor of another vision in terms of complementarities, which tends to show that innovation and export form a virtuous circle that creates synergies. This chapter, therefore, puts into perspective the operational difficulty of implementing an innovation–export relationship in business support with regard to the theories mobilized in the academic world. The underlying complexity of the innovation–export relationship thus encourages a paradigm shift away from the causalist system towards a vision in terms of synergies favoring emergence.

1.1. The innovation–export link: a controversial debate

1.1.1. *In the industrial world: a compartmentalized vision*

When you look at the numbers, it turns out that innovative SMEs (i.e. companies driving both product/process/service innovation and organizational and business innovation) are more likely to be engaged in global markets than non-innovative companies. A report on the behavior of European SMEs (FedEx 2015) shows that fast-growing SMEs were almost twice as likely to export as declining or stagnant SMEs. At the European level, a survey from the OECD (2009) shows that internationally active SMEs are three times more likely to introduce new products or services than their purely domestic counterparts, and they grow more than twice as fast. From 2012 to 2014, innovative companies were more numerous among exporting structures than non-exporters, with the gap being greatest in the case of product and process innovations. Exporting SMEs thus introduced twice as many product and process innovations as non-exporting SMEs (OECD 2018). Outside Europe, this trend also appears to be similar. For example, in 2011, it was reported that 60% of Canadian exporting SMEs introduced at least one type of innovation (product, process, organization or marketing) versus only 35% of non-exporters (Seens 2015). Thus, the numbers speak for themselves, and it appears that small innovative companies have a greater international presence and vice versa.

This observation suggests the existence of a close relationship between innovation and export activities, which has indeed been identified both in the scientific literature and at the institutional level. Moreover, for several years now, there has been a tendency to propose a coupling of innovation and export support systems (European Commission 2007). This is what Love and Roper (2015) highlight in their study, insisting on the importance of considering the systems jointly to maximize their joint benefits. They also recommend offering coordinated support with a single agency responsible for both innovation and export. However, this type of study is still not widespread. Indeed, it would seem that despite the potential benefits of an innovation–export coupling in support of SMEs, few export support systems integrate an innovation dimension. They are generally concentrated almost exclusively on aspects related to international trade.

These observations are indeed confirmed by the field. A comparative study integrating a hundred or so internationalization[1] support systems worldwide (Enjolras *et al.* 2015) highlights several observations. First of all, these systems are of different natures. They offer companies several types of support: awareness/information, financial support, promotion of the information, financial support, network promotion or individualized support.

For the remainder of this study, we define the following notations:

– I: represents the type of support "provision of information";

– F: represents the type of "financial" support;

– N: represents the type of support "networking";

– In: represents the type of "individualized" support.

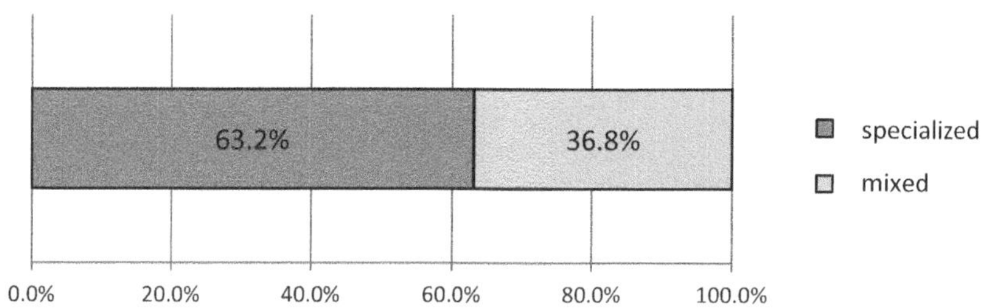

Figure 1.1. *Distribution of mixed/specialized systems (Enjolras* et al. *2015)*

It is important to note that a single facility may offer several types of support. Each facility may, therefore, appear in more than one category. Figure 1.1 shows the distribution of specialized programs, that is, those offering only one type of support, compared to mixed programs offering two or more distinct types of support. A clear majority of export support systems offer specialized support (63.2%).

Figure 1.2 shows the distribution of systems by the four types of support considered. In this figure, mixed systems appear in more than one category, as they offer several types of support. For example, 50% of the systems surveyed provide information to businesses. Next, 41% of the systems offer

1 This comparison mainly includes support systems for internationalization (and therefore not exclusively for export) aimed at SMEs, although some are also aimed at all types of companies.

financial support. Finally, systems offering individualized support or promoting networks represent 35.8% and 27.4%, respectively.

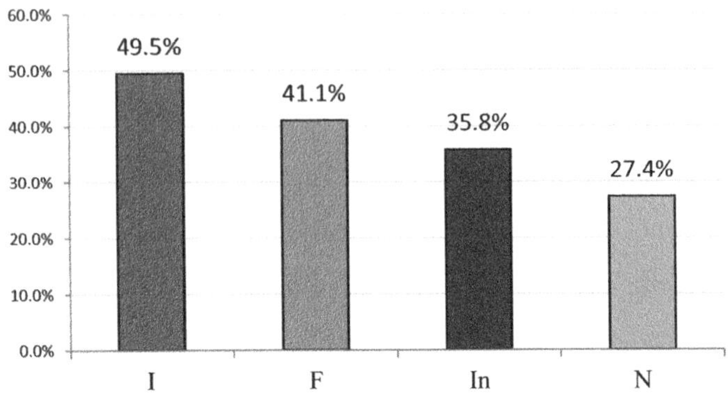

I: Information distribution
F: Financial support
In: Individualized support
N: Networking

Figure 1.2. *Distribution of systems according to the four types of support (Enjolras* et al. *2015)*

In view of these results, it appears that the support systems for internationalization are mainly oriented towards the dissemination of information and financial support. This result is interesting because it highlights the strategic points on which the support organizations act as a priority. Thus, it is a question of rather punctual support, aiming either at sensitizing the SME to the problems of the international markets or at proposing financial assistance to them, allowing them to increase their available resources in the short term. This is in line with the conclusions of Seringhaus and Rosson (1990), who consider the measures proposed by export support organizations to be mainly incentive-based. In addition, most of the support systems are specialized in a particular type of support. This specialization potentially multiplies the number of actors involved in business support and can make access to the systems more complicated.

As regards the inclusion of innovation in export support systems, the majority of these systems appear to be compartmentalized. Of the hundred or so systems identified, only 11% include an innovation dimension. The tendency to combine export and innovation support systems identified in the literature is, therefore, still not widespread at the global level, from an operational point of view.

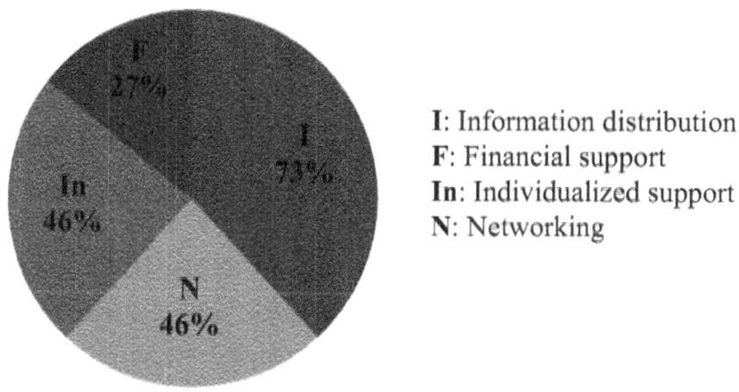

Figure 1.3. *Distribution of joint innovation–export support systems by the four types of support (Enjolras* et al. *2015)*

According to Figure 1.3, within the joint innovation–export support systems, information distribution (I) again seems to be the most important type of support (73%). However, network promotion (N) becomes much more important (46%). It is possible to explain this increase, as the ability to network is a very important impact factor both for innovation performance (Chesbrough 2003; Nieto and Santamaría 2010; Zeng *et al.* 2010) and internationally (St-Pierre *et al.* 2011; Child and Hsieh 2014; Hohenthal *et al.* 2014), and especially for SMEs. It, therefore, seems relevant to propose support acting on this dimension in particular. On the other hand, financial support (F) loses much of its importance (27%) in joint innovation–export support systems. Personalized support, on the other hand, increases in relation to the values reached by purely export-oriented systems. Finally, the study highlights the systems, including an innovation dimension, that tend to combine several types of support; they are mostly mixed (see Figure 1.4).

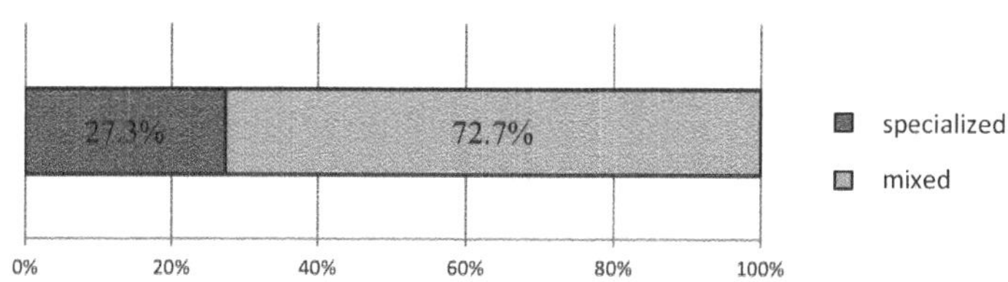

Figure 1.4. *Distribution of joint innovation–export support systems by specialization or not (Enjolras* et al. *2015)*

The profile of joint innovation–export support systems is, therefore, different from that of "traditional" support systems. The latter are oriented towards incentive and rather short-term support, whereas joint systems seem to favor networking and individualized support. They tend to offer several different types of support and seem to provide SMEs with diversified and longer-term contributions through the acquisition of sustainable resources and skills.

However, it is important to specify that "traditional" support systems, which are more short-term-oriented, are not less suitable for supporting SMEs than "joint" systems, which are oriented towards the acquisition of long-term skills. A study by Francis and Collins-Dodd (2004) highlights the fact that the impact of support systems is not the same depending on the degree of international involvement of SMEs. The reason is simple: the needs are not the same. Indeed, depending on their degree of internationalization (Kotabe *et al.* 2002), SMEs mobilize different resources, skills and strategies, and the obstacles they encounter are not the same. The role of support systems must, therefore, vary according to this degree of internationalization (Catanzaro *et al.* 2013). Thus, the first stage of international commitment requires that SMEs be made aware of the benefits of and approach to internationalization in order to consider their launch on foreign markets. The "traditional" support systems, and therefore incentives, are perfectly appropriate for a degree of a low level of commitment. On the other hand, the more SMEs increase their level of commitment to internationalization, the more they need to acquire resources and strategic skills. The joint innovation–export support systems, therefore, seem more appropriate in this case, but in view of the low level of commitment, they are not as appropriate. This common vision represents a way of encouraging the development of a new type of business model. This joint vision is indeed an interesting way of managing the complexity of companies and takes on its full importance in the particular context of SMEs, for which the available resources are limited (Szczepanski 2016).

1.1.2. *In the academic world: a causalist vision questioned*

1.1.2.1. *Self-selection or learning-by-exporting?*

The innovation–export relationship is a very important area of research in the current scientific literature. The dominant paradigm under which this relationship is studied can be described as causal, as it emphasizes a causal relationship between innovation and exporting (Love and Roper 2015). Innovation would have a positive effect on exporting and, similarly, exporting would impact innovation. Traditionally, two theories coexist: "self-selection" and "learning-by-exporting", and each promotes an opposite direction of causality. Is it innovation that impacts export or export that impacts innovation?

The self-selection theory is based on an assumption that innovation makes it easier for companies to reach the international market (Roper and Love 2002; Monreal-Pérez *et al.* 2012; Boso *et al.* 2013; Dai *et al.* 2019; Ribau *et al.* 2019). This is the majority accepted theory in the scientific community. It is therefore supported by a large number of publications. Thus, according to this theory, innovation confers a competitive advantage to the company, which allows it to acquire a higher general performance and to improve the optimization of its resources. Innovation thus allows companies to be more competitive in foreign markets and facilitates their internationalization. Innovation thus appears to be a necessary condition for exporting (see Figure 1.5).

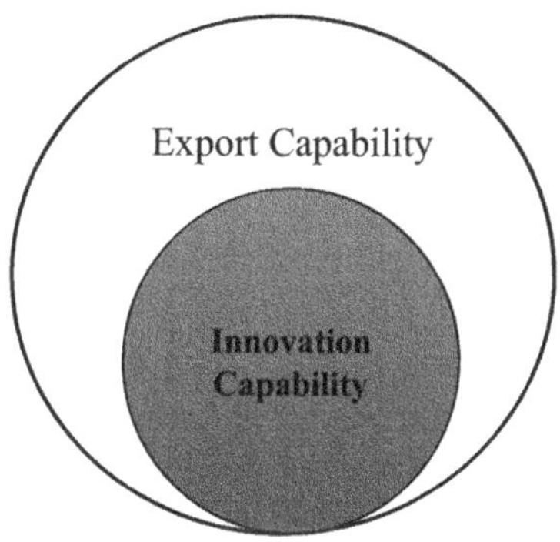

Figure 1.5. *Graphical representation of the self-selection theory*

Several empirical studies have been carried out to test this theory with panels of companies of various sizes, sectors of activity and geographical areas. For example, Pla-Barber and Alegre (2007) validate self-selection through a study of 120 French companies of all sizes from the biotechnology sector. Similarly, Roper and Love (2002) also studied the impact of innovation on the international performance of German and British companies. The main conclusion is that the nature of the impact of innovation on exports depends on the context of the company (country of origin, size and sector of activity).

These findings are confirmed by Altomonte *et al.* (2013). It is important to note, however, that in both of these studies, innovation is considered only from the perspective of product innovation.

Thus, in addition to the context in which the company operates, the type of innovation considered also seems to have an impact on the nature of the innovation–export link. Indeed, van Beveren and Vandenbussche (2010) emphasize the importance of the correlation between product innovation and process[2] innovation. Introducing a new product or process separately does not significantly encourage exporting, but introducing both simultaneously has a stronger positive impact (Becker and Egger 2013). Thus, companies prepare for entry into foreign markets by reducing costs (process innovation) and increasing product quality (product innovation). Caldera (2010), however, puts forward somewhat different results, indicating that, in general, innovation promotes exporting in companies, but that process innovations have a smaller impact than product innovations. This result can be explained by the fact that product innovation allows for strong differentiation from competitors in foreign markets as well as better product quality, which provides a greater competitive advantage than process innovation, whose objective is rather to reduce costs.

Concerning SMEs in particular, the innovation–export link is also validated by various articles (Cassiman *et al.* 2010; Cassiman and Golovko 2011; Higón and Driffield 2011) in the context of product innovation. Le Roy and Torrès (2001) propose an additional element by proving that the positive impact of product innovation on the international activities of SMEs does not depend on the geographical area of the target market. The hypothesis that the context impacts the innovation–export relationship is thus qualified by these results.

In general, while self-selection is a theory that is widely accepted in the literature, it is also regularly discussed. Bellone and Guillou (2013) analyze the innovation–productivity–export link. The main result is that innovation is not the only cause of productivity and export gains. Other factors must be taken into account. On the other hand, Deng *et al.* (2014) consider that the link between

2 "Process innovation" means the implementation of a new or significantly improved production or delivery method (including significant changes in techniques, equipment and/or software). By extension, process innovation also refers to new improvements in the way products are delivered to customers.

innovation and export can be negative and that it is necessary to take into account the heterogeneity between companies. They show that, for Chinese industrial companies, innovation has a positive impact on export intensity, but its impact is not necessarily positive for survival in foreign markets. Finally, Oura *et al.* (2015) also test the impact of innovativeness on the export performance of Brazilian SMEs. They argue, however, that innovativeness is mainly considered a key factor in improving companies' performance in foreign markets, but little attention is paid to inter-country experience as an equally important factor as innovativeness. They prove that international experience has a greater impact on export performance than innovative capability.

Thus, self-selection appears to be a widely accepted theory considering innovation as a necessary condition for SMEs to export. However, many studies highlight the fact that it is above all a necessary condition, but not sufficient, to ensure the sustainability of the international activities of SMEs. This is highly dependent on factors linked to the type of innovation considered, the context in which companies evolve and their heterogeneity. Moreover, this theory is counterbalanced by another theory emphasizing the importance of international experience: learning-by-exporting.

The theory of learning-by-exporting is based on the assumption that exports lead to improved innovation within a company, as well as its performance more generally (Kafouros *et al.* 2008; Golovko and Valentini 2014; Fassio 2018; Di Cintio *et al.* 2019). The discovery of a foreign market allows the company to acquire a large amount of information and knowledge. This acquired knowledge pushes the company to adapt and therefore innovate to maximize its success both in this new market and in its domestic market. It is, therefore, a contributing factor to an organization's innovation capability (see Figure 1.6).

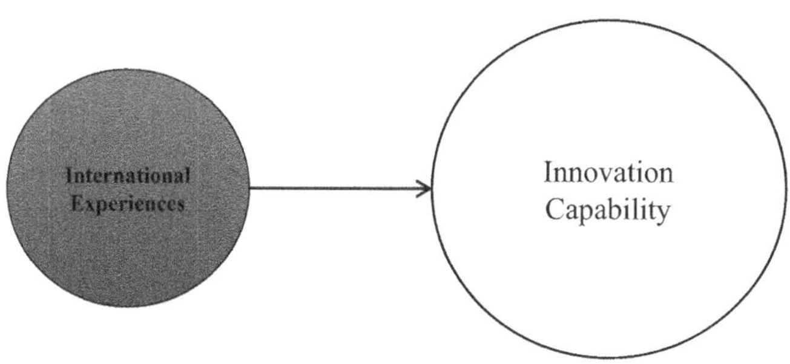

Figure 1.6. *Graphical representation of learning-by-exporting*

Lileeva and Trefler (2010) take this view. Their findings indicate that in Canadian industrial companies, access to foreign markets favors innovation and, in particular, product innovation. The learning-by-exporting theory also seems to depend on the type of innovation considered. Thus, international experience could have a greater or lesser impact on the company's innovation capability, depending on the type of innovation undertaken.

Thus, the effects of learning-by-exporting would only be visible under certain conditions. Kafouros *et al.* (2008) give the main implications of exporting for innovation capability and appropriation of innovation. The notion of threshold is discussed: exporting only positively influences innovation (and more particularly the return on investment of innovation) if the company's international activities reach a certain threshold, called the "degree of internationalization".

Learning-by-exporting, as a mirror theory of self-selection, is also discussed by many authors and appears not as a necessary condition for innovation but as a catalyst whose effects are multiplied 10-fold under certain conditions. While the question of the type of innovation always seems crucial, the notion of context is only very rarely addressed as a differentiating factor. These two theories, therefore, coexist in the literature, both reflecting a certain vision of the innovation–export relationship, based on causal thinking in terms of impact.

1.1.2.2. *A two-way relationship: towards a virtuous circle*

While the majority of studies of the innovation–export nexus focus on a definite direction of causality (self-selection or learning-by-exporting), several authors have tested the hypothesis that causality between innovation and export can be bidirectional. This means that self-selection and learning-by-exporting theories could coexist as a virtuous circle (Cassiman and Golovko 2011; Halilem *et al.* 2014; Zehir *et al.* 2015; Ayllon and Radicic 2019).

However, these investigations show results that are sometimes surprising. For example, Damijan *et al.* (2010) propose an empirical test of the two-way innovation–export relationship in Slovenia. The results confirm that exporting encourages process innovation, but the other hypotheses are not significant enough to be verified. The results seem to hold only for medium and large companies. It is interesting to note that the results of this study are rather contrary to the elements put forward by other authors studying one or the other of these two theories: product innovation does not seem particularly significant, and the SME context does not seem to be conducive to a bidirectional relationship. Similarly, Monreal-Pérez *et al.* (2012) study the bidirectional link between innovation and exporting in Spanish industrial companies. They test both hypotheses simultaneously: self-selection and learning-by-exporting. Their results show that exporters develop more innovation activities and invest more in R&D. They develop and accumulate more knowledge and skills than exporters. They develop and accumulate more product innovations. According to them, innovation has a positive impact on exports. However, the learning-by-exporting hypothesis is not validated in their study. One explanation: geographical and cultural distance, which favors learning-by-exporting, does not play a major role in this study, as Spain largely exports to culturally close European Union countries. This reinforces the place of the degree of internationalization as a trigger for the "international experience" catalyst. Exporting to culturally close countries reflects a low degree of engagement in international markets and thus minimizes the effects of learning-by-exporting. Thus, these results do not call into question the bidirectional link between innovation and exporting but rather characterize it conditionally.

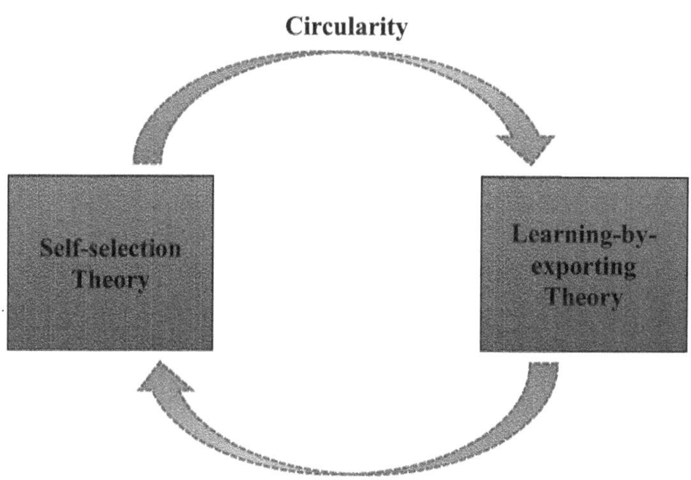

Figure 1.7. *Graphical representation of the bidirectional innovation–export relationship*

Some authors shed additional light on this potentially bidirectional relationship. Halilem *et al.* (2014) propose a study of Canadian industrial

SMEs and empirically validate the bidirectional link between innovation and internationalization. This study considers product and process innovation, as well as import and export. It, therefore, adopts a broader scope than learning-by-exporting. Following this logic, Damijan and Kostevc (2010) propose another study in which they investigate the theory of learning-by-trade in Spanish companies (also including importing and exporting, not just exporting). This study led to the proposal of a sequence: import/innovation/export/innovation (1) or export/innovation/import/innovation (2). Sequence (1) was chosen because the empirical results seem more significant. Importing encourages companies to innovate (product and process innovation, but especially product innovation) and to start exporting. Finally, exporting is introduced by innovation and ultimately leads companies to launch new products, but not necessarily new processes. This is also true for small companies.

Thus, innovation seems to have a positive impact on export performance (especially product innovation), and exports also seem to improve the innovative capacity of SMEs with a specific temporality. They point out that self-selection and learning-by-trade can coexist as a temporal sequence. Finally, Filipescu *et al.* (2013) propose a study that concerns the reciprocity between exporting and innovating in the Spanish context. Exporting is measured in two categories: the extent of exporting activity and its intensity. Innovation is represented by product and process innovation and by R&D intensity. The main conclusion is that the impact of innovation on export is not an exact mirror of the impact of export on innovation. There is a mutual reinforcement of export and innovation (Filatotchev and Piesse 2009), but this reinforcement takes a different form depending on the direction considered. This study provides an interesting perspective on the impact of one activity on the other. It highlights that the link between innovation and exporting does not seem to be limited to a simple mirror effect.

Thus, the bidirectional causal relationship between innovation and export seems to exist under certain conditions (temporality, degree of commitment to international business) and according to differentiating factors (company size, type of innovation, context). These observations and the complex thought they suggest concerning the nature of the link between innovation and export pave the way to other hypotheses that allow us to go beyond the cause-and-effect relationship and move towards an alternative vision.

1.1.2.3. *Complementarity: an alternative way out of the causalist paradigm?*

Some studies concerning the innovation–export link propose to go further in the reflections carried out by adopting a different vision of the links between these two activities. These authors try to show that in the case of SMEs, innovation and exporting are complementary: if a commitment is made to one of these activities, it facilitates the commitment to the other via synergy effects.

The results of Golovko and Valentini (2011) show that Spanish manufacturing SMEs that invest in both innovation and exporting enjoy better growth than those that invest in either innovation, exporting, or neither. The return on investment in one activity increases with the level of performance of the other activity. However, Ayllon and Radicic (2019) found that while complementarity between innovation and exporting exists, it subsists only in contemporaneous effects. Their results suggest no evidence of a link between past product and process innovations and current export activity. Thus, temporality again appears to be a key factor to consider.

The academic view of the innovation–export relationship paves the way for many hypotheses, both in terms of determining factors and in terms of the vision to be adopted. It is, therefore, difficult to identify a real consensus concerning the link between innovation and export. While the majority of studies consider this link in causal and directional terms, certain forms of alternative relationships are also envisaged, putting forward the notions of a virtuous circle (bidirectional relationship) or complementarities. Generally speaking, and whatever the vision adopted, this relationship seems to be more or less strong depending on the context in which the company evolves, its size, its degree of commitment to international business and the type of innovation considered. For SMEs, it would seem that product innovations are very largely discriminating. They appear before they enter the foreign market (self-selection), as well as later and in a more important way (learning-by-exporting). Thus, the notion of temporality, or even of temporal sequence, also seems essential. This review of the literature thus highlights that, in the context of SMEs, innovation cannot be considered as a simple condition for exporting. Similarly, exporting cannot be limited to a prerequisite for innovation. The relationship between these two activities is much more complex than that and deserves an in-depth analysis that goes beyond a simple cause-and-effect relationship.

1.2. Towards a paradigm shift

SMEs, like all forms of organization, are confronted with complex problems, that is, problems with numerous interactions, in which different frames of reference/systems of thought coexist, and for which the interweaving of interpersonal relations, techniques and managerial practices is indispensable. Innovation and exporting are examples among many others. Moreover, it has been shown previously (see section 1.1.2.3) that these two activities have strong links, which seem to go further than a simple cause-and-effect relationship. However, the study of this link largely remains confined to an academic issue, adopting a dominant causalist thinking and giving rise to numerous hypotheses that have not yet found a consensus. In practice, therefore, the link between innovation and export remains rare and difficult to operationalize in the support offered to SMEs.

The objective of this section is, therefore, to propose a new paradigm adapted to the operational context of SMEs and offer an alternative to the analytical vision of treating innovation and export separately within companies. The aim is to promote a systemic vision, taking into account the interactions and complementarities between these two entities. To do this, it is necessary to rely on the theoretical foundations of the systemic and complex approach and then to apply the main precepts to the management of innovation and export in the context of SMEs.

1.2.1. *Moving from analytical thinking to complex thinking*

1.2.1.1. *The strength of systems theory*

The development of Western thought and science is based on a rationalist and analytical tradition. It is considered a universal reference. However, this superiority of the rationalist tradition is largely questioned by the systemic approach. This approach is based on the notion of system, which, according to Joël de Rosnay (1975), can be defined as "a set of elements in dynamic interrelation, organized according to a goal". It is a conceptual tool capable of helping to solve a complex problem (Yatchinovsky 2012).

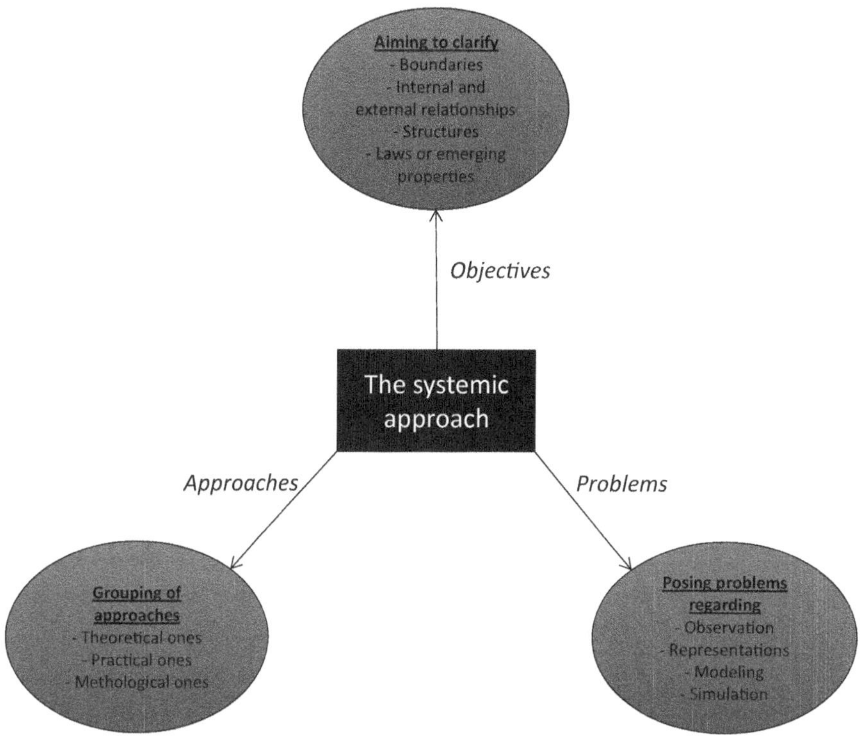

Figure 1.8. *Definition of the systemic approach, inspired by (Durand 2006)*

The systemic approach emerged from three precursor scientific movements (Durand 2006):

– structuralism, introducing the notion of structure as a basis for reflection. This movement is used in particular in the human sciences (linguistics, anthropology, psychology, etc.);

– cybernetics, coming from the Greek *kubernesis*, reflecting the action of directing, of governing. Cybernetics, or the "science of governance", represents a crossroad that has seen the emergence of numerous discoveries from various scientific fields. It has contributed, along with structuralism, to the emergence of the concept of organization and has fostered the exchange of ideas between specialists from various disciplines;

– information theory, which developed at the same time as cybernetics, and which was even considered as a part of the latter before seeing its field of research widen considerably.

Thus, in 1985, the French college of systemics gave a definition of it schematized by Figure 1.8.

1.2.1.2. *A systemic rationalism opposition*

The systemic approach is opposed to the rationalism expressed in Descartes's *Discourse on Method* (1637). It is based on four fundamental precepts:

> The first was never to accept anything as true unless I knew it to be true, that is to say, to carefully avoid haste and prevention [...]. The second was to divide each of the difficulties that I would examine into as many parts as I could and would be required to better resolve them. The third was to conduct my thoughts in order, beginning with the simplest and easiest to understand objects, and then to ascend little by little, as if by degrees, to the knowledge of the most complex [...]. And the last one to make everywhere such complete enumerations and such general reviews that I would be sure not to omit anything.

Rationalist precepts	**Systemic precepts**
Evidence	Relevance (in relation to the researcher's findings)
Reductionism (analysis)	Globalism (taking the system's environment into account)
Causalism (linear reasoning)	Teleology (system's behavior research)
Exhaustiveness	Aggregativity (for a simplifying representation)

Table 1.1. *Comparison of rationalist and systemic precepts (source: Le Moigne (1994))*

In his book, Le Moigne (1994) contrasts Descartes's four precepts with the precepts of the systemic approach (see Table 1.1):

– relevance (as opposed to evidence) consists of considering something as true in relation to explicable purposes. The perception of an object changes according to the intentions of the modeler;

– globalism (as opposed to reductionism) challenges the supremacy of analysis. It is about considering an object as a part included and active in a larger whole, an environment. It is about putting forward the notion of emergence by considering that the whole is more (or less) than the sum of its parts, according to Aristotle's maxim;

– teleologism (in opposition to causalism) consists of questioning the causalist thinking according to which the world is endowed with a structure, an order, and this structure incorporates invariant laws of cause and effect. Causalist thinking proposes reasoning in terms of necessary and sufficient conditions and in terms of linearity. The teleological precept, on the contrary, proposes a reflection on the behavior and the finalities of the object as well as on the resources that it mobilizes. It is a question of considering that the relation between two elements is not a simple causal action of A on B; it comprises a double action of A on B and of B on A;

– aggregation (as opposed to exhaustiveness) challenges the principle of exhaustiveness, which is difficult to achieve in reality. This precept proposes to accept the differences and variability of situations, not by "omitting" elements but by voluntarily and explicitly aggregating them.

These four precepts, therefore, call into question the rationalist and analytical approach in favor of a systemic and complex vision. It is, therefore, on these four precepts that we will base the proposal of a new paradigm for the understanding and joint management of innovation and export within SMEs.

1.2.1.3. *A key concept: complexity*

In addition to the four precepts presented above, systems thinking is based on four fundamental concepts (Durand 2006):

– interaction (the relationship between two elements is not limited to a simple causal action);

– globality (the whole is more than the sum of its parts);

– organization (arrangement of relationships between components that produces a new unit with qualities that its components do not have);

– complexity, which we will explore further in this section.

The concept of complexity is actually a paradigm in itself. It should not be confused with complication. Complexity is a set of heterogeneous constituents inseparably associated and organized as well as the uncertainties, indeterminations and random phenomena associated with them. The complication, as for it, represents a system composed of many elements more or less in disorder but whose principle of composition is simple.

Thus, complex thought consists of substituting the paradigm of simplification, including principles of disjunction (separating what is linked) and/or reduction (unifying what is diverse), with a paradigm including principles of conjunction that allow us to distinguish without disjoining and to associate without reducing (Morin 1994).

Edgar Morin describes three principles for thinking about complexity:

– The dialogical principle: considers that two elements are not simply juxtaposed but necessary to each other. They can even be perceived as complementary and antagonistic at the same time (order and disorder, for example). A dialogical relation is a "fundamentally complex relation, that is, at the same time complementary, competing, antagonistic and uncertain" between two notions (Morin 1977). However, the notion of dialogic is not necessarily limited to the relation between two notions. In the third volume of *La Méthode*, Morin (1986) defines the dialogical principle as "the complex association (complementary/competing/antagonistic) of instances [not of 'two instances'] necessary together for the existence, the functioning and the development of an organized phenomenon".

– The principle of organizational recursivity, or the whirlpool process: each moment of the whirlpool is both the product and producer. A recursive process is one in which the products and effects are both the causes and producers of what produces them. This principle is an idea that breaks with the principle of cause and effect. What is produced returns on what produces it in a cycle that is itself self-constituting. We can speak of a virtuous circle.

– The hologram principle: amounts to considering that the part is in the whole but that the whole is in the part. Pascal (1976) illustrates this principle in the following way: "I cannot conceive the whole without conceiving the parts, and I cannot conceive the parts without conceiving the whole." This principle is part of recursive logic (what we acquire as knowledge of the parts returns to the whole and vice versa), which is itself related to dialogical logic in a sense.

Thus, to be open to complex thought is to seek to connect in order to construct meaning rather than to give in to the ease of fragmentary analyses (Le Moigne 2007). It is necessary to "join in order to understand", whereas, on the contrary, the simplification exercise requires "separating to understand", which implies a reduction and/or a disjunction of reality. Thus, complex thinking, and all that it implies, represents a fundamental notion for thinking about the innovation–export relationship in terms of complementarities and synergies. This is a considerable contribution compared to disjunctive thinking because it highlights unifying and common elements without merging the whole. It is a matter of joining without confusing and distinguishing without disjoining.

1.2.2. *Theoretical framework: articulation of mobilized theories*

In order to support a complex vision of the relationship between innovation and export in SMEs, it is necessary to build a relevant theoretical framework articulating different scientific theories on which to base our reflection. This theoretical framework is mainly based on the theory of industrial organization and its SCP (structure, conduct, performance) model. From this basis of reflection, several scientific theories will be presented in order to complete the SCP model and to adapt it to the particular case of innovative and exporting SMEs.

1.2.2.1. *The theory of industrial organization: the SCP model*

This theory is based on the SCP paradigm. Between 1960 and 1970, the authors behind this paradigm (Mason 1959; Bain 1968) considered that the structure of the market influences company conduct, which determines their performance. Market structure refers to environmental factors: supply, demand, competitive intensity, the existence of barriers to entry, standards and regulations, etc. Business conduct describes what companies do and how they do it (positioning, pricing, R&D, distribution strategies, etc.). Finally, performance refers to the results of industrial sectors and companies (profitability, growth, efficiency, technical progress, etc.). This first school of thought is traditionally called the "Harvard School". From the 1970s onwards, however, the SCP model was called into question, particularly the causal and linear relationship between structure, conduct and performance on which it was based (Tirole 1988). A new school of thought, therefore, appeared: the new industrial organization. The main contribution of this school of thought is to consider that the company can modify its environment through strategic decisions (Uzunidis 2016). Various feedback effects are then added to the Harvard School model (see Figure 1.9), making the SCP paradigm more dynamic and integrating a more complex vision of the interactions presented.

This theory provides an interesting basis for our research. By modifying its conduct, a company can, on the one hand, modify the structure of its own market, and, on the other hand, improve its performance in this same market. The modifications of its conduct are then based on strategic decisions influencing its internal organization. However, this SCP model needs to be further developed to adapt it to the specific context of our research work. We therefore propose to examine the different S, C and P dimensions in the light of different scientific theories in order to propose a complete and relevant theoretical framework (see Figure 1.9).

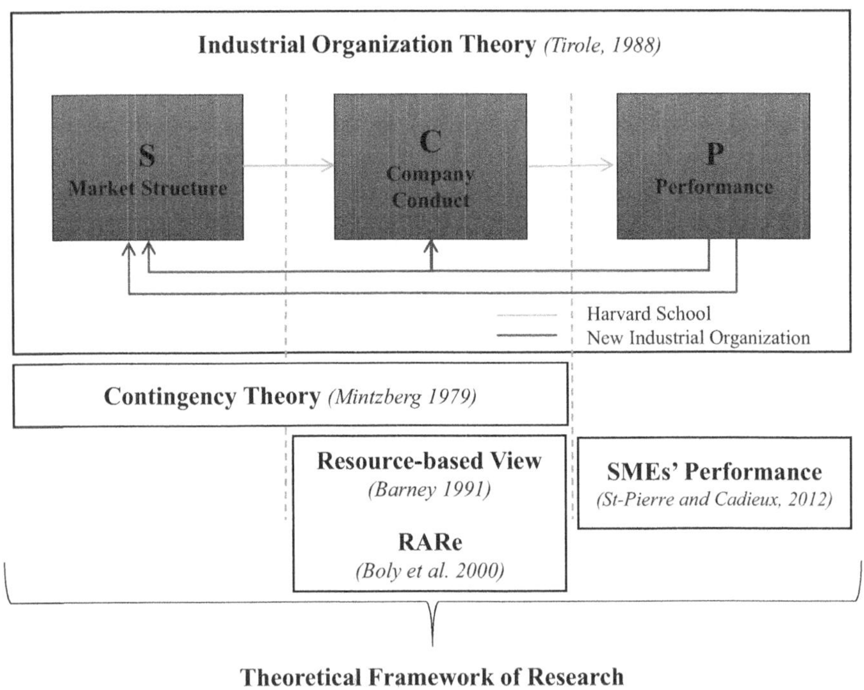

Figure 1.9. *Construction of the theoretical framework of the research. For a color version of the figure, see www.iste.co.uk/enjolras/innovation.zip*

1.2.2.2. *The relationship between the structure and conduct: contingency theory*

In the context of our research, the contingency theory appears as a complement to the theory of industrial organization presented in section 1.2.2.1, particularly when we are interested in the relationship between the structure of the market (or the environment) and the conduct of the company (or organization). This school of thought considers that there is no such thing as a good organization *per se*. Henry Mintzberg, the main representative of the contingency school, states that the structure of an organization depends on both its own characteristics and the nature of its environment (Mintzberg 1979). There is, therefore, no universal structure that adapts to all situations. A "good" structure must be adapted to its environment, and an environment shapes the organizations that compose it.

Based on the scientific literature, different factors of contingency can be identified, reflecting contextual elements that can push companies to adopt certain behaviors.

Contingency factors	Description	Sources
Environment/geographical area	Public policies, regulatory context, political/economic stability	Mintzberg (1979), Choi and Lim (2017), van den Heiligenberg *et al.* (2017) and Urbinati *et al.* (2018)
Centralization/decentralization	Power relations, decision-making process	Mintzberg (1979) and Liu *et al.* (2018)
Structure of the organization	Size, age	Mintzberg (1979), Forés and Camisón (2016), Akinwale *et al.* (2018) and Belas *et al.* (2018)
Market orientation	Competitiveness, internationalization, industry, technological intensity	Mintzberg (1979), Thornhill (2006), Love and Roper (2015), Korab and Koudelkova (2016), Tidd and Thuriaux-Alemán (2016) and Crowley and Jordan (2017)

Table 1.2. *Contingency factors from the literature*

Thus, contingency theory sheds light on the S–C part of the SCP model proposed by the new industrial organization. The conduct of a company evolves to respond to the constraints of its specific market. Its internal regulatory systems must therefore be as varied as the environment with which it must deal. To overcome the constraints of its environment, the company must adjust its conduct by making strategic decisions that allow it to set up a coherent and specific internal functioning that will enable it to improve its performance and, finally, to impact the structuring of its own market.

1.2.2.3. *Acting on the conduct of SMEs: a vision in terms of resources and activities*

After having examined the relationship between structure and conduct, we propose to focus on the conduct of companies and more particularly that of SMEs. To do so, we propose to introduce a theory that is particularly well suited to the study of small structures: the resource-based view (Brulhart *et al.* 2010).

Resource-based view is a model from strategic management (Collis and Montgomery 1995). It first appeared in the work of Penrose (1959) and focuses on the way in which competitive advantage is generated through a combination of resources present within the company (Dhanaraj and Beamish 2003).

Strategic management is based on a theoretical framework according to which a company creates a competitive advantage by implementing a strategy that exploits its own strengths while responding to opportunities in its environment. This strategy avoids external threats and neutralizes internal weaknesses (Barney 1991). Two models exist (see Figure 1.10):

– environmental models of competitive advantage: an external analysis of the opportunities and threats facing the company;

– the resource-based model: an internal analysis of the company's strengths and weaknesses.

Strategic management thus seems to be in line with the contingency theory presented in section 1.2.2: a company adapts to the characteristics of its environment. However, strategic management has an important limitation for our study. Environmental models of competitive advantage assume that resources and strategies are broadly the same across companies in the same group (e.g. by industry) (Porter 1998). Heterogeneity is not taken into account.

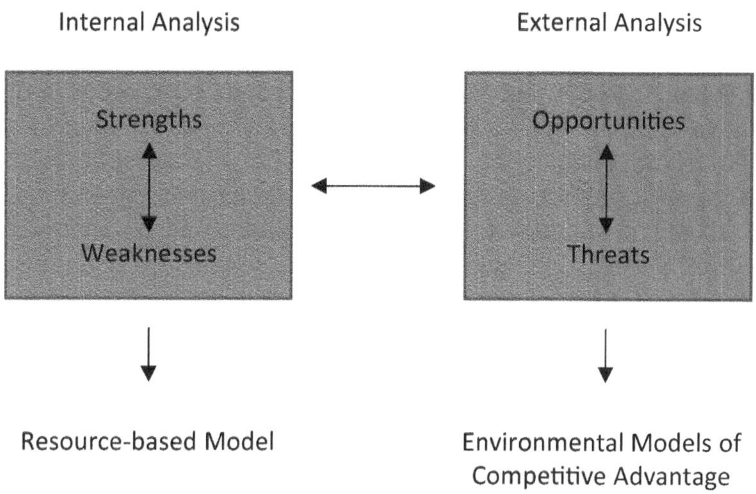

Figure 1.10. *The two models of strategic management (Barney 1991)*

The resource-based model, on the other hand, takes into account the heterogeneity and disparity of resources and strategies across companies. It, therefore, eliminates the limitation identified in the environmental models of competitive advantage. For this reason, we propose to study the conduct of companies from the perspective of resources alone to take into account the heterogeneity of companies.

According to the resource-based view, companies can be considered as a set of resources and these resources are heterogeneously distributed within companies (Teece *et al.* 1997). A company's resources are its tangible and intangible assets, and competencies are related to the ability to combine these resources (Julien 2005). Some of these resources, known as "strategic", are considered to be the foundations of competitive advantage in the domestic and international market (Barney 1991). According to Barney, a strategic resource must be valuable, scarce, not easily transferable or imitable and not substitutable. A resource is valuable when it allows the company to design and introduce strategies that improve its performance while satisfying the needs of consumers. A strategic resource must be scarce for the company's current and potential competitors. If a resource is valuable but possessed by a large number of companies, it will be exploited in the same way by each of them, which will prevent the creation of any competitive advantage. Similarly, a strategic resource must be inimitable. Valuable and scarce resources can still be imitated by competitors if they need them. The non-replicability of a strategic resource is, therefore, a key point in creating competitive advantage. Finally, a strategic resource must not have a substitute. No resource should be strategically equivalent, as this would allow competitors to develop a similar strategy and break the competitive advantage created by the strategic resource in question (López Rodríguez and García Rodríguez 2005). Thus, a company must promote the acquisition and mobilization of strategic resources in order to adapt to the threats of its environment or to seize certain opportunities. The resource-based view thus represents a complementary theoretical basis to the SCP model, and it seems particularly adapted to the context of SMEs that encounter difficulties related to their overall lack of resources.

To go further, we propose to consider the link between resources and activities. For SMEs, the mobilization of strategic resources requires, on the one hand, identifying them, and, on the other hand, being able to exploit them through the implementation of specific activities that allow the desired result to be achieved. These strategic activities represent proof of a company's ability to use the resources it has at its disposal. Having the resources is not enough; we must be able to exploit them. Thus, we propose to complete the resource-based view by introducing the RARe models.

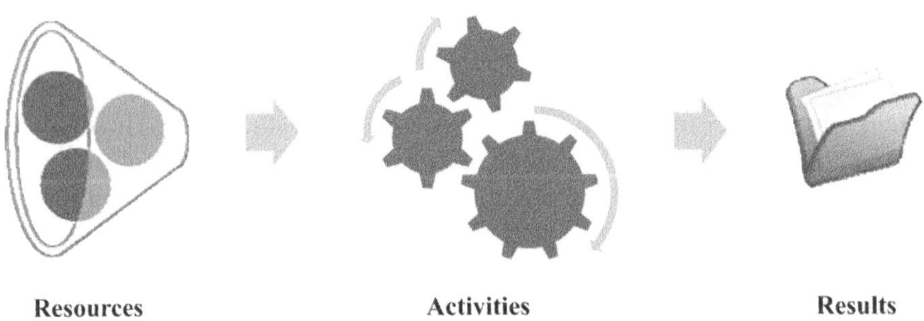

Figure 1.11. *The RARe model (Ben Rejeb 2008)*

RARe is the abbreviation for resource–activity–results. These models are based on a systemic approach that consists of analyzing, for a particular actor, the resources used to carry out activities and the result produced (Boly 2008). The RARe makes it possible to link the resources to be mobilized, the way they are used (activities) and the envisaged objective (results) (see Figure 1.11).

We, therefore, propose to apply the RARe model to SMEs' innovation and export capabilities. To improve their innovation and export capabilities, SMEs must modify their behavior and, therefore, the activities they implement to better identify and exploit their strategic resources in order to achieve a tangible result. For example, a company wishing to export to a new market must know its competitors in that market. According to the RARe model, the tangible result it wishes to achieve would be a list of potential competitors in the market in question. To do this, the company must, for example, set up a competitive intelligence activity. It must therefore mobilize resources such as a network of business leaders, IT tools, support systems, etc.

The RARe model emphasizes the importance of a global vision in the form of a triptych of resources, activities and results. These three elements are interrelated and make it possible to affirm that, in order to achieve an objective that it has set for itself, a company must not only have access to resources but also know how to mobilize them and use them correctly. It must therefore modify its own routines in order to adapt its behavior and gain in performance while adapting to the environment in which it evolves. Through this RARe vision, we, therefore, choose to follow in the tradition of Schumpeter (1934) via the capability approach, which describes what the company can do and how it seeks to carry out innovation and international activities to ensure continuity over time. From this perspective, the entrepreneur is an actor of change, and the company achieves an outcome via the mobilization of multiple resources responsible for the implementation of practices/routines reflecting the adoption of a specific behavior (Zawislak *et al.* 2014).

1.2.2.4. *The notion of performance for innovative and exporting SMEs*

In order to propose a complete theoretical framework, we need to consider the third element of the SCP model: the notion of performance.

Traditionally, corporate performance is measured in terms of financial indicators. However, this approach has been questioned for many years (Kaplan and Norton 1996). The performance of companies is, in fact, multi-criteria. In particular, performance indicators must be linked to the objectives and strategies of companies in order to be relevant and representative (St-Pierre and Cadieux 2012). According to Berrah (2013), the expression of performance is a step in an improvement process, in accordance with the precepts of the Deming wheel. This expression of performance can take different forms: a measurement or an evaluation. Performance measurement is an expression of the achievement of an objective by comparison with an observed measure. It is expressed, for example, through steering or monitoring indicators. Performance evaluation is an expression that also results from a measurement compared to the objective but related to a specific interval (between 0 and 1, for example). It incorporates a form of satisfaction on the part of the decision-maker in the light of the measures achieved, and gives an interpretation in relation to a global vision or reference framework. It is expressed this time through strategic, global and structural indicators. Performance evaluation can be used in the context of a diagnosis, in which case it can be used to explain the performance achieved in terms of effectiveness (whether or not objectives were achieved) and efficiency (use of the resources allocated). In the context of an optimization process, it makes it possible to visualize how to improve the achievement of objectives.

Our research work is based on the context of innovative and exporting SMEs. Numerous performance indicators and evaluation methods have been identified for both innovation (number of patents, investment in R&D, etc.) and export (export sales, etc.) (Muller *et al.* 2005; Boutary *et al.* 2013). However, the performance indicators used are mainly quantitative and oriented towards economic performance. However, in the specific case of SMEs, the multiplicity of performance indicators is even greater. St-Pierre and Cadieux (2012) identified four types of objectives in terms of performance through the study of more than 300 Quebec SMEs:

– personal performance (recognition, quality of life, assets, etc.);

– economic performance (growth, profit, international, etc.);

– sustainable performance (meeting customer needs, maintaining jobs, financial health, etc.);

– social performance (quality of life of employees, reputation of the company, etc.).

The notion of performance in SMEs, therefore, seems very complex, and the interest of adopting a multi-criteria vision seems undeniable.

In view of this particular context, we therefore propose to adapt the SCP model by integrating into the notion of performance its multi-criteria character, which is particularly characteristic of the case of SMEs. Moreover, a key notion of this research work is that of the improvement of the performance of SMEs and thus of the evaluation of their performance. According to Berrah's work, the evaluation is either part of a diagnosis or part of an optimization process. In this research work, we have chosen to reconcile the two by proposing a support tool dedicated to SMEs, in the form of a diagnosis to assess their innovation and export capabilities and then to optimize it through the identification of ways to improve. On the other hand, the stronger an SME's innovation and export capability, the better it will perform, according to our research. We do not seek to quantify the performance of SMEs in terms of results (patents, sales, etc.); we evaluate the potential of companies through the evaluation of their internal routines (their behavior) (Galvez 2015).

1.2.2.5. *The articulation of different theories: the SCP model revisited*

The different theories presented in this section lead to a theoretical framework on which our research is based. First, the industrial organization theory highlights the links between the structure of the market, the behavior of the SME and its performance. By performance, we mean here the innovation and export capabilities. Then, according to the contingency theory, to improve its performance, a company must respond to the constraints imposed by its market by making adjustments to its behavior or its internal structure. These adjustments involve the identification and acquisition of strategic resources (resource-based view), which must then be exploited through activities (in the sense of Schumpeter) that lead to a tangible result (RARe model).

The articulation of these four theories allows us to come up with a revisited SCP model (see Figure 1.12) so that it is suitable for the specific context of SMEs, on the one hand, and for the study of their innovation and export capabilities, on the other hand.

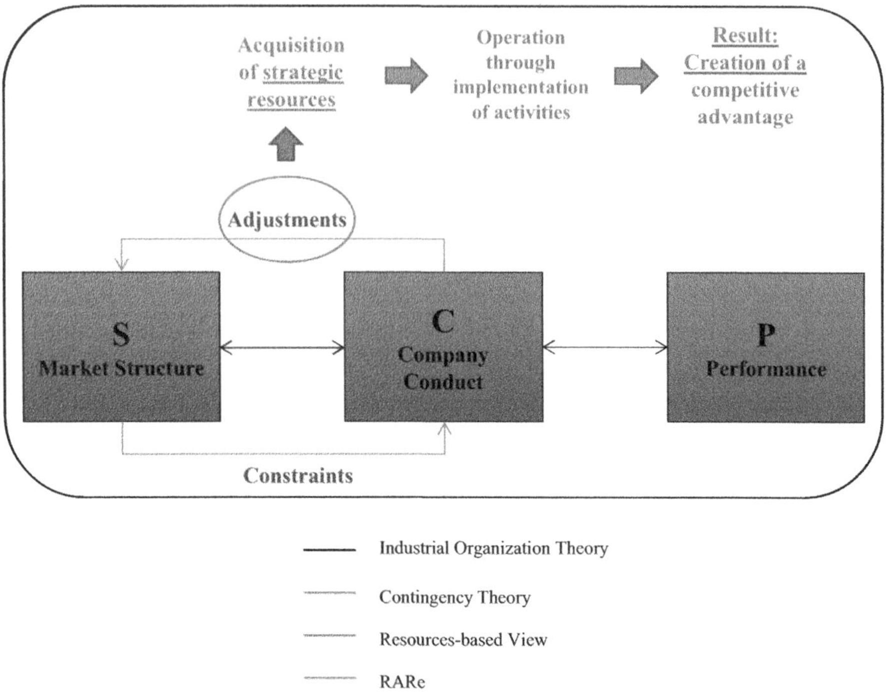

Figure 1.12. *The SCP model revisited: theoretical framework. For a color version of the figure, see www.iste.co.uk/enjolras/innovation.zip*

1.2.3. *The application of the complexity paradigm to SME innovation and export activities*

The previous sections of this chapter (see sections 1.2.1 and 1.2.2) have made it possible to put forward the fundamental theories and notions that serve as a basis for creating a new paradigm for thinking about the innovation–export relationship. Thus, it was possible to propose a new point of view on this relationship based on complementarity and complex thought. Based on a paradigm shift initiated in the literature on the innovation–export relationship, this paper proposes an alternative to the analytical vision that consists of treating innovation and exporting separately within companies by favoring instead a systemic vision that considers the existing synergies between these two activities. The contribution of this work lies in the systemic vision chosen to analyze this relationship within SMEs and in the mobilization of an appropriate theoretical framework to support and model this complex vision based on the SCP model.

1.2.3.1. *Towards the creation of a common innovation–export space*

As demonstrated earlier (see section 1.1), the innovation–export relationship is generally thought of as disjointed in the literature. Innovation and export are considered two separate activities, although they have a mutual impact on each other. On the contrary, in this section, we propose considering innovation and export as two complementary activities that create synergies. This new paradigm thus aims to replace the commonly accepted analytical view with a complex view of this relationship.

Analytical thinking isolates what it separates and obscures what connects and differs. Complex thought, on the other hand, makes it possible to join while distinguishing.

In his book *Introduction à la pensée complexe*, Morin (1994) said:

> Join the cause and the effect, the effect will come back to the cause, by feedback, the product will also be productive. You will distinguish these notions and you will join them at the same time.

Based on this quote, we propose to apply the principles of dialogism and recursivity to the innovation–export relationship. Thus, the proposed paradigm considers innovation and export as the two poles of the same dialogical and recursive duality. That is, these two poles form a virtuous circle (recursivity) within which they are united without the duality being lost in this unity (dialogism).

The meeting of these two complementary poles creates a common space conducive to the emergence of synergies. Thus, through this paradigm, innovation is not only a prerequisite or a necessary condition for exporting and vice versa. We propose to consider innovation and export as two complementary activities.

The notion of complementarities can take different forms (Morin 1977):

– interactions;

– links establishing a common area;

– associations and combinations of complementary activities;

– informational communications.

The studies cited above (see section 1.1) have highlighted the interactions and exchanges of information between innovation and export. These are indeed interactions in the form of reciprocal actions that innovation and export exert on each other (Durand 2006). These reciprocal actions include exchanges of information, and this is particularly true in the case of learning-by-exporting, where information from international markets impacts the innovation process. The complementarity between innovation and exporting thus seems to be proven in terms of interactions and informational communication.

However, the vision we support proposes to go further in the complementarity by integrating into the innovation–export relationship a common space that can be considered as an interface between these two activities. This common space represents the activities that an SME must carry out as a priority to simultaneously create a value in terms of innovation and export (see Figure 1.13).

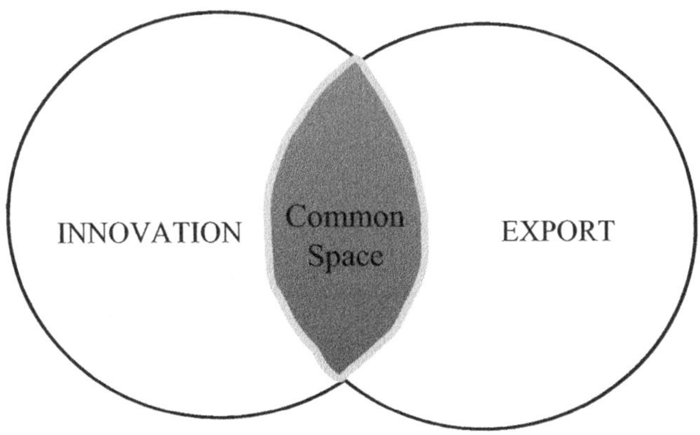

Figure 1.13. *Theoretical positioning*

We, therefore, hypothesize an enhanced complementarity in the form of a linkage that establishes a common part. In the particular context of SMEs, for which the lack of resources is a particularly important problem (Szczepanski 2016), this vision seems particularly relevant, as it is based on the assumption that it is possible to exploit an innovation–export synergy in order to reduce the effort needed to reach a defined goal. By acting in this common space, companies potentially trigger a single lever that has a simultaneous impact on their innovation and export activities and produces a synergistic result that requires less effort than two separate actions. This common space is therefore composed of the activities/routines that an SME must implement to create a value simultaneously in terms of innovation and export. It, therefore, reflects a behavior based on a dialogical and recursive logic for which the development of specific activities/routines allows the mobilization of joint resources, skills and knowledge that are at the origin of synergies between innovation and export. This is how the notion of emergence appears. From the innovation–export coupling, more than a simple addition of activities or resources specific to one or the other is born.

Thus, this paradigm is mainly based on a basic notion of the systemic approach: complexity. It applies two fundamental principles: dialogism and recursion. Finally, it is based on a vision in terms of complementarities, leading to the emergence of a common space whose main property is to reduce the effort required to increase the performance of an SME simultaneously in terms of export and innovation.

1.2.3.2. *What does this paradigm contribute to SMEs?*

Most of the problems SMEs have to deal with are complex. Innovation and export are among them because they are "disorganizing" and directly affect the value creation process. They call into question the company's strategy in relation to its environment. We can speak of denaturation in the sense of Torrès and Julien (2005). Denaturation, for the study of SMEs, considers that "small size" does not necessarily mean "small structure". Thus, a company with a small workforce can nevertheless adopt formalized management methods, a decentralized management, define an anticipatory strategy and expand its market internationally. It then becomes more like a "miniature large company" by adopting practices that are generally characteristic of large companies. Innovation and exporting are activities that encourage this denaturation of SMEs. By opening their market to the international market or by piloting innovation projects, they modify their organization and their management methods by turning to a formalization and structuring of their internal processes.

At first glance, SMEs may find it more difficult to solve complex problems such as innovation and exporting, among others, due to the constraints imposed by their size. But this is not necessarily the case.

They do not necessarily face more difficulties than other types of organizations (Blackstone and Cox 1985) because their flexibility and their proximity to their employees are powerful assets. However, other difficulties specific to SMEs in dealing with complex problems can be identified (Schmitt *et al.* 2002; Okręglicka *et al.* 2015; Moeuf *et al.* 2018). For example, the omnipresence of the leader and the centralization of management can be penalizing. Problems are generally addressed by a single person who is the leader, and this forces him or her to perpetually evolve in complexity. On the other hand, the short-term vision and the lack of formalization of the company's strategy are also sources of uncertainty. According to Morin (1994), complexity calls for strategy. An SME manager must have a long-term vision while managing the day-to-day running of the company. However, in general, the short-term vision is privileged in SMEs because of the need to manage urgent problems. Thus, the lack of formalization of the strategy, as well as the centralized management within the SME, hinders the management of complex situations. Problems are generally considered separately, and rarely in relation to the organization's interactions.

In the particular case of innovation and export, a lack of a clear, long-term strategic vision can lead to a compartmentalized management of these two activities. In the same way, centralized management and decision-making can make it difficult to take into account the existing interactions between innovation and export. However, a complex vision of innovation and export management that emphasizes a common space can be a real advantage for SMEs. Indeed, the coupling innovation–export allows us, on the one hand, to reinforce the coherence and the homogeneity of the company strategy. This opens the way to the initiation of a global vision by "decompartmentalizing" these two activities and by taking into account the inter-relationships that characterize them. Within SMEs, this opening up is made possible and can be facilitated by their flexibility and their proximity to the staff. This seems to be particularly adapted to their context. On the other hand, the emergence of a common space highlights the existence of common activities, skills and resources for innovation and export. By encouraging companies to act on these common elements as a priority, an emergence effect appears. The notion of emergence is defined by the appearance of properties of a system that are new compared to the properties of its components considered separately (Morin 1977). In this particular case, we do not consider that the whole is more than the sum of its parts; we consider that the whole is less than the sum of its parts in terms of the efforts associated with the rise in performance. In fact, acting on the activities, resources and skills common to innovation and export enables us to activate a single lever (a common element), which has repercussions on two activities (innovation and export). The effort required to improve performance is, therefore, lower than if the company had used two levers (one for innovation and one for export). This is an optimization of available resources and, therefore, a response to the main difficulty encountered by SMEs, both in developing innovation and in sustaining their international activities.

2

Joint Innovation–Export Best Practices

In view of the scientific positioning exposed in Chapter 1, this chapter aims to identify and characterize the common space between innovation and export, in order to highlight the joint activities on which SMEs must act in priority to improve their performance, both in terms of innovation and export.

The objective is, therefore, first of all, to identify which activities are specific to innovation and which are export-related. The aim is to create a set of best practice frameworks to characterize the innovation and export areas separately so that they can then be better linked together. As these frameworks are built on a similar logic and structure, it is then possible to merge them in order to characterize the common innovation–export space in the form of joint best practices.

2.1. The construction of a theoretical frame of reference

The first step in developing the joint practice framework is to determine the basis for assessing innovation and export capabilities. Both of these capabilities have been extensively studied and have been validated and tested using several assessment models. In addition, it was established earlier (see section 1.2.3) that innovation and exporting share common characteristics and factors. This common model is therefore based on the assumption that it is possible to establish relationships between the assessment of the two capabilities.

2.1.1. *Identifying innovation practices: the potential innovation index (PII)*

The rapid changes in today's industrial world, as well as the globalization of markets, are pushing companies to constantly renew themselves in order to react more quickly to the developments they face (Taneja *et al.* 2016). As a result, innovation capability management has become a strategic priority for companies and institutions, as illustrated by the recent publication of the international standard on innovation management systems (ISO 56002 2019).

This context has led many researchers to study models to understand, evaluate and improve the innovation capability of companies. Among the first authors to work on this type of model, Chiesa *et al.* (1996) proposed a model based on the evaluation of seven processes: concept generation, product development, process innovation, technology acquisition, human and financial resources, systems and tools, and leadership. In the same vein, Adams *et al.* (2006) conducted an exhaustive literature review focusing on the identification of practices that characterize the innovation capability of companies. They identified seven main practices: resource management, knowledge management, innovation strategy, organizational culture and structure, portfolio management, project management and marketing. Similarly, Guan *et al.* (2006) propose a model oriented towards technological innovation by evaluating seven dimensions: learning, R&D, production, marketing, resource exploitation, organizational capacity and planning strategy.

In the specific context of small companies, Pierre and Fernandez (2018) propose a review of the literature on the impact factors of innovation capability. They provide a comparison of several evaluation models highlighting aggregated dimensions. For example, Terziovski (2010) emphasizes that the innovation strategy, the structure of the company, its customer/supplier relationships, its innovation culture and, finally, its technological capabilities have an impact on its performance. Forsman (2011) proposes an exploration of the innovation capability of SMEs, regardless of their sector and size, and identifies six main factors: knowledge gathering and exploitation, entrepreneurial capabilities, risk management, networking, market orientation, customer knowledge and change management.

Thus, the latest generation of innovation capability assessment models, like ISO 56002, focuses on identifying and assessing internal practices that characterize a company's innovation management system. However, there is still no consensus as to which practices or evaluation frameworks are the most appropriate. This can be explained by the complex nature of innovation (Edison *et al.* 2013). It can indeed be considered either as a new or modified product, service, process, business model or organization (ISO 56002-2019) and seems to be impacted by the context, location (Choi and Lim 2017), size and age of the company (Belas *et al.* 2018), its business sector (Tidd and Thuriaux-Alemán 2016) or its technological orientation (Thornhill 2006). Moreover, studies on benchmarks for assessing innovativeness have mainly agreed on the assumption that models based on practices that integrate a multifactor view better address the cross-cutting characteristics of innovation (Hagedoorn and Cloodt 2003). Indicators should therefore be structured on the basis of a multi-criteria approach involving various sub-processes (Chiesa *et al.* 1996).

This last consensus justifies the choice of our theoretical framework, based on the PII developed by the research team on innovative processes (ERPI) of the University of Lorraine (France). The PII appears to be a relevant indicator for our study because it is based on a multi-criteria structure that makes it possible to understand innovation in the form of internal practices present within the organization of companies. Due to the standardized and generalizable character of its practice framework, it has been tested and validated both theoretically (Boly 2004; Ben Rejeb *et al.* 2008; Boly *et al.* 2014) and empirically on French, Argentinean and Chilean SMEs operating in various sectors (Sepulveda *et al.* 2010; Galvez *et al.* 2013).

It is based on six innovation practices, selected from the scientific literature (see Figure 2.1): creativity, product/service design, human resource management, strategy, project management and knowledge management (Corona 2005).

Each of these practices is composed of several activities, which themselves include a number of observable phenomena. An observable phenomenon can be defined as the tangible and verifiable result of a routine activity within the company, requiring the allocation of resources (time, money and personnel) to be carried out. Observable phenomena thus play the role of indicators allowing the evaluation of the innovation activity considered. If these observable phenomena are present within the company, the activity they characterize can then be considered as mastered.

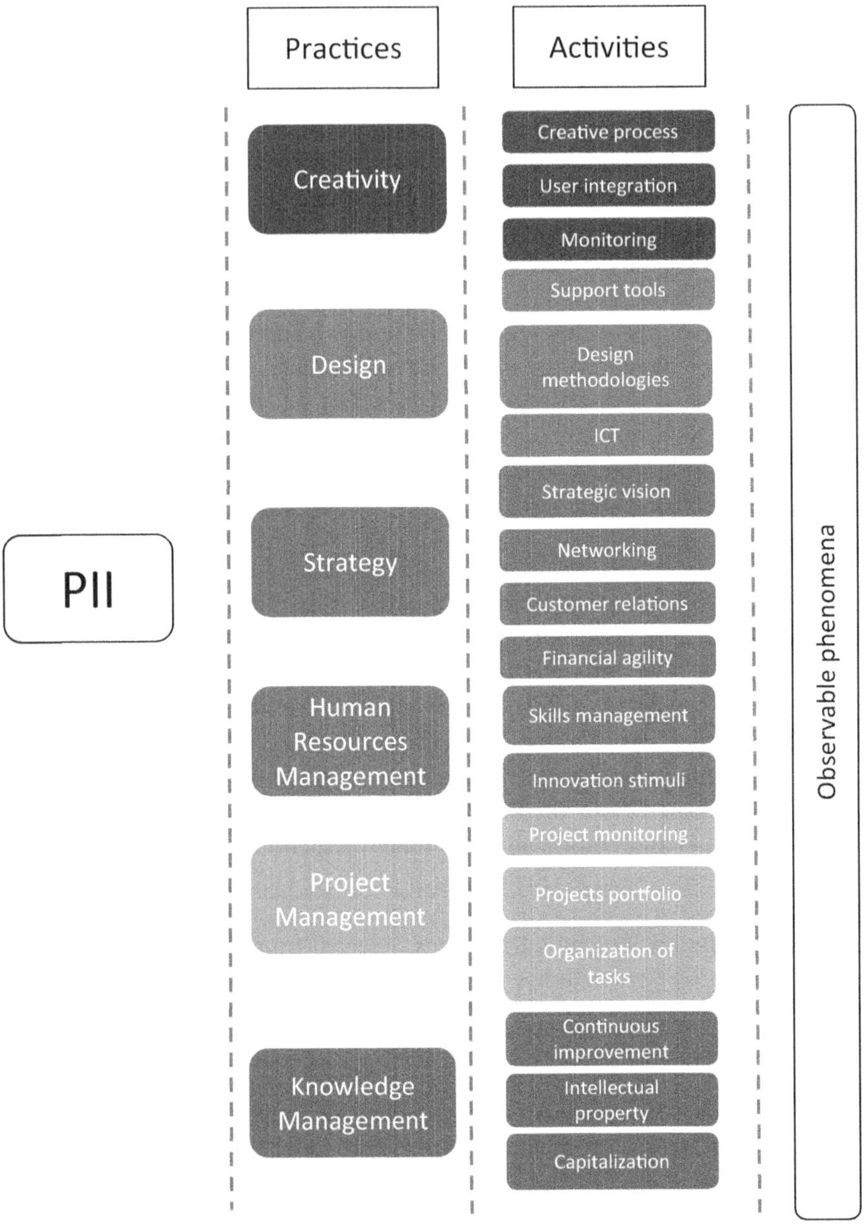

Figure 2.1. *Benchmark of best innovation practices: the PII. For a color version of the figure, see www.iste.co.uk/enjolras/innovation.zip*

2.1.2. *Identification of export practices*

In the scientific literature, export models generally propose a result-oriented view where performance is measured either by mainly economic indicators (export sales, growth, market share, margin, etc.) or by market-oriented indicators (number of products exported, number of exporting countries, etc.) (Katsikeas *et al.* 2000). Thus, different models have been developed to evaluate export performance through the resources mobilized and the behavior of the company (Dhanaraj and Beamish 2003) or by taking into account external or environmental factors related to the context or the target market of the company (Katsikeas *et al.* 2000).

For example, Morgan *et al.* (2004) develop an empirical model in which they include factors such as resources, capabilities, competitive strategy, competitive advantage, foreign competitiveness and performance as drivers of the export process. Martineau and Pastoriza (2016) define the concept of international participation in terms of two elements, export propensity and export intensity. The latter incorporates factors such as human capital, relationships with customers and governments, relationships with suppliers and competitors, and market knowledge and engagement. Anil and Shoham (2017) explore the internal and external barriers that affect exporting, the motivations to export and the associated benefits. Oliveira *et al.* (2017) study how performance is affected by export market dynamism, information sharing and goal alignment. Dhanaraj and Beamish (2003) determine that size and technological intensity are good predictors of a company's export strategy. Navarro-García *et al.* (2016) validate the inter-relationships between human resources and managerial attitudes, competitive intensity, export commitment, strategic behavior, export performance and the existence of an export department.

Thus, as with innovation, export performance has been considered through a set of internal factors and processes. However, a significant difference seems to appear with the innovation models because, unlike the latter, the export-related models strongly focus on external or contextual factors. However, they also emphasize that internal skills and practices are levers for improving a company's export capability. Thus, there are recurring factors in the models that can be considered relevant to assessing a company's export capability. Among these, strategy defines the company's roadmap for managing resources and allocating them to foreign markets. Human resource management should also be considered, particularly the way they interact with the environment in which the company operates. Finally, relations with customers and suppliers, as well as the company's knowledge and learning process, appear as significant factors.

On the other hand, the operational implementation of these factors is often little explored (Katsikeas *et al.* 2000; Anil and Shoham 2017), and the proposed models are often confined to a descriptive level. Thus, it is difficult to extract best practices from them in the same way as that proposed in the case of innovation capability assessment. This is why the first phase of this study consisted of identifying in the scientific literature the factors linked to exporting that can be expressed as internal practices. Different dimensions representing the best export practices were then put forward and characterized in the form of activities and observable phenomena in a manner similar to the structure of the PII presented earlier (see section 2.1.1).

These theoretical data were then confronted with the business world through 20 interviews conducted with international SME managers, as well as with experts in SME internationalization (researchers, consultants, advisors, etc.). According to Glaser and Strauss (1968) and Yin (2013), the validity of data from qualitative methods such as interviews relies on the notion of theoretical saturation, which is directly related to the number of cases. Eisenhardt (1991) states that the number of interviews to be conducted depends on the existing knowledge on the topic under study. She adds that the ideal number is between 4 and 10 for reasons of data volume control. In the context of the interviews conducted, the aim is to enrich the theoretical data from the literature. The existing knowledge on the studied theme is, therefore, relatively important, which makes it possible to limit the number of interviews to be carried out. However, our sample includes three different types of interlocutors (exporting SMEs, researchers, coaches). This is why we sought above all to reach theoretical saturation, that is, the number of interviews from which incremental learning is minimal (Hlady-Rispal 2016), that is, from one interview to the next, we observed facts that had already been observed. This theoretical saturation finally emerged after 19 interviews were conducted.

These interviews made it possible to refine the theoretical data identified in the literature in order to obtain the most realistic model possible. Eight practices were thus validated, and the associated activities and observable phenomena were completed, thus forming a benchmark for evaluating the export capability of SMEs: the potential export index (PEI).

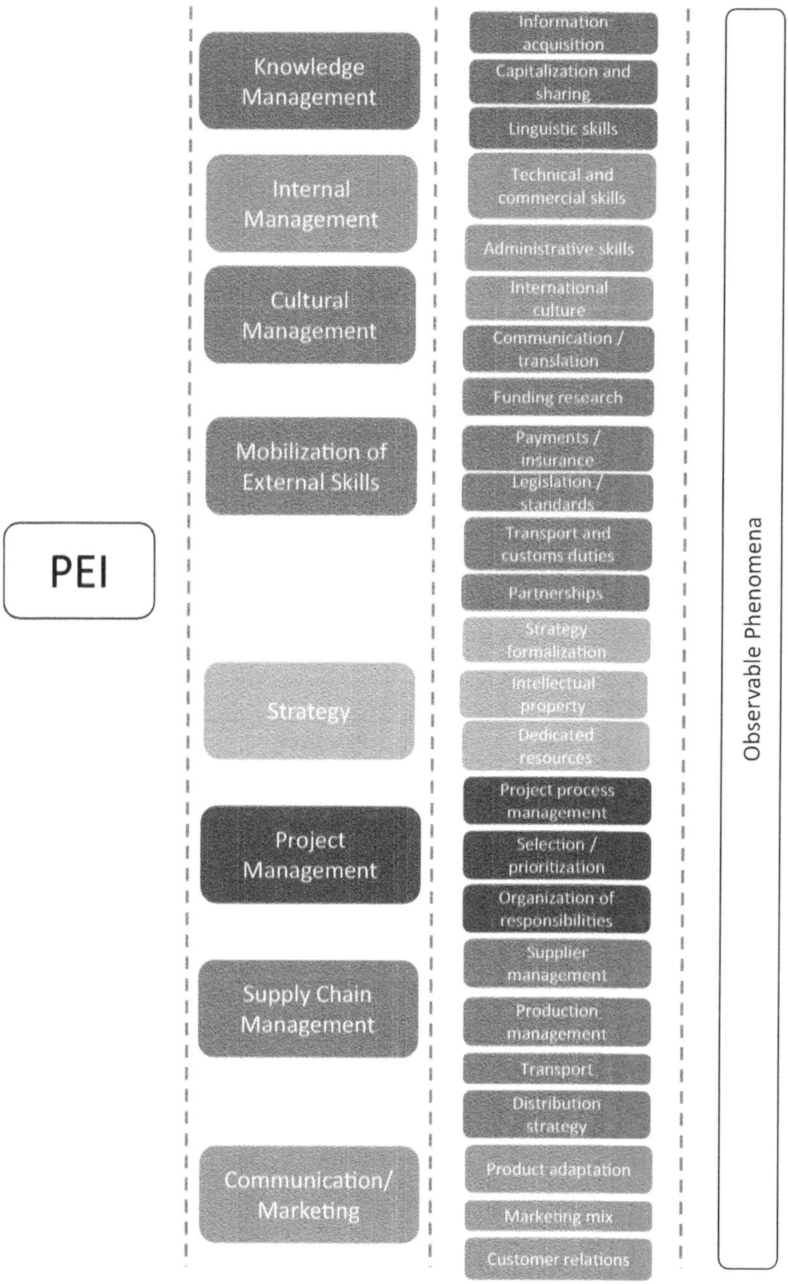

Figure 2.2. *Best export practice benchmark: the PEI. For a color version of the figure, see www.iste.co.uk/enjolras/innovation.zip*

2.1.3. *Towards a joint reference system*

In order to move towards the proposal of a joint innovation–export reference framework, the objective of this section is to characterize the common space grouping together with the joint innovation–export activities resulting from the innovation (PII) and export (PEI) reference frameworks proposed previously (see sections 2.1.1 and 2.1.2). However, this characterization goes further than a simple addition of activities common to innovation and export. It is a matter of identifying joint innovation–export activities, which require a combination and not an addition. We consider a common activity as an activity belonging to the innovation (export) framework and which is coupled to another activity belonging to the export (innovation) framework. The identification of joint innovation–export activities thus amounts to highlighting several pairs of activities that retain their respective membership of one or other of the framework. On the other hand, a joint activity is a combination of several common activities. It is a matter of associating, combining and joining groups of common activities to create emergences and thus propose a new framework characterizing a common innovation–export space that goes further than a simple intersection between two spaces.

<table>
<tr><th colspan="3">Innovation</th><th colspan="3">Export</th></tr>
<tr><th>Practices</th><th>Activities</th><th>Code</th><th>Practices</th><th>Activities</th><th>Code</th></tr>
<tr><td rowspan="3">Creativity</td><td>Creative process</td><td>I1</td><td rowspan="2">Knowledge management</td><td>Acquisition of information and knowledge</td><td>E1</td></tr>
<tr><td>User integration</td><td>I2</td><td>Capitalization and sharing</td><td>E2</td></tr>
<tr><td>Monitoring</td><td>I3</td><td rowspan="3">Management of internal skills</td><td>Linguistic skills</td><td>E3</td></tr>
<tr><td rowspan="3">Design of new products</td><td>Support tools</td><td>I4</td><td>Technical and commercial skills</td><td>E4</td></tr>
<tr><td>Design methodologies</td><td>I5</td><td>Administrative skills</td><td>E5</td></tr>
<tr><td>ICT</td><td>I6</td><td>Management cultural aspects</td><td>International culture</td><td>E6</td></tr>
<tr><td rowspan="4">Strategy</td><td>Strategic vision</td><td>I7</td><td rowspan="4">Mobilization of external skills</td><td rowspan="2">Communication/ translation</td><td rowspan="2">E8</td></tr>
<tr><td>Networking</td><td>I8</td></tr>
<tr><td>Customer relations</td><td>I9</td><td>Funding research</td><td>E9</td></tr>
<tr><td>Financial agility</td><td>I10</td><td>Payments/insurance</td><td>E10</td></tr>
</table>

Innovation			Export		
Practices	**Activities**	**Code**	**Practices**	**Activities**	**Code**
Human resource management	Skills management	I11	Mobilization of external skills	Legislation/ standards	E11
	Innovation stimuli	I12		Transport and customs duties	E12
Project management	Project monitoring	I13		Partnerships	E13
	Project portfolio	I14	Strategy	Formalization of the international strategy	E14
	Organization of tasks	I15		Intellectual property	E15
Knowledge management	Continuous improvement	I16		Dedicated resources	E16
	Intellectual property	I17	Project management	Project process management	E17
	Capitalization of knowledge	I18		Selection/ prioritization	E18
			Supply chain management	Organization of responsibilities	E19
				Supplier management	E20
				Production management	E21
				Transport	E22
				Distribution strategy	E23
			Marketing	Product adaptation	E24
				Marketing mix	E25
				Customer relations	E26

Table 2.1. *Key terms: specific practices/activities*

2.1.3.1. *The analysis of similarities*

First, a similarity analysis was carried out (Degenne and Vergès 1973) in order to identify activities common to innovation and export by comparing two-by-two innovation activities with exporting activities. To gain in precision, the comparison was made at the level of observable phenomena. Indeed, for this research, we define the similarity of two activities as the presence of common elements between them. Two activities are considered similar if they have at least one observable phenomenon in common.

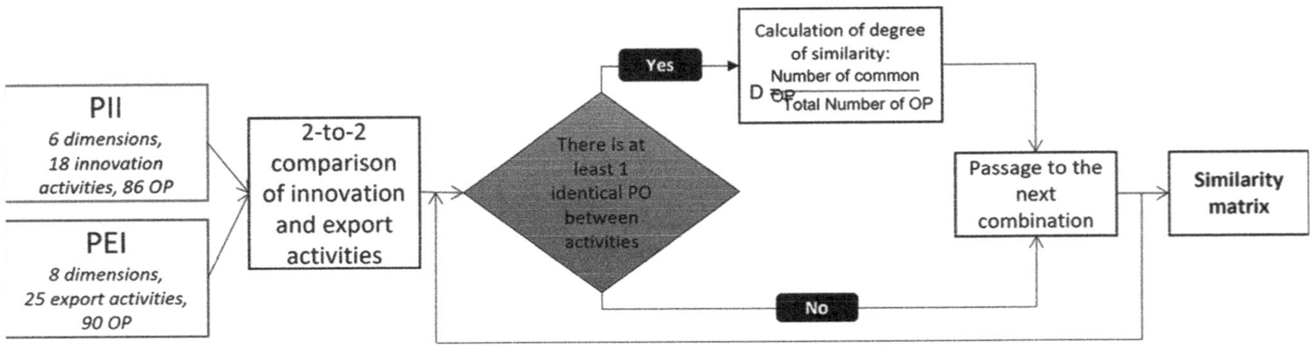

Figure 2.3. *Methodology adopted for the similarity analysis. For a color version of the figure, see www.iste.co.uk/enjolras/innovation.zip*

For each pair of activities identified as similar, a degree of similarity is calculated (see Figure 2.3). Let I be an innovation activity, comprising n observable phenomena, and E an export activity, comprising p observable phenomena. When comparing I and E, we are interested in the number of common observable phenomena k among p and n. The degree of similarity between I and E *is* therefore considered to be equal to $\frac{k}{(p+n)}$.

The main result of the comparison is a similarity matrix that allows us to visualize the pairs of activities common to innovation and export as well as the strength of their similarity (via the calculation of their degree of similarity). This matrix is presented in Figure 2.4.

	E1	E2	E3	E4	E5	E6	E8	E9	E10	E11	E12	E13	E14	E15	E16	E17	E18	E19	E20	E21	E22	E23	E24	E25	E26
I1	0.07	0.08																							
I2	0.07	0.08																	0.14			0.13	0.63		
I3	0.56	0.19																							
I4																									
I5																									
I6		0.10																							
I7		0.08											0.80		0.14		0.13					0.13		0.38	
I8	0.23						0.50			0.20	0.33	0.78							0.50		0.14	0.43			
I9		0.17																					0.63		0.43
I10								0.40							0.25										
I11		0.18	0.43	0.43	0.20							0.11			0.17			0.29							
I12						0.78																			
I13		0.14											0.08		0.33	0.64									
I14													0.60		0.14		0.63								
I15		0.25													0.14			0.75							
I16	0.07	0.77														0.30									
I17														0.40											
I18	0.06	0.93											0.08			0.17									

Similarity degree
Between 0 and 0.25
Between 0.25 and 0.50
Between 0.5 and 0.75
Between 0.75 and 1

Figure 2.4. *Similarity matrix. For a color version of the figure, see www.iste.co.uk/enjolras/innovation.zip*

The similarity matrix obtained gives an indication of the composition of the common innovation–export space through the identification of common activities with a greater or lesser degree of similarity[1]. However, this similarity matrix highlights pairs of common activities, but not joint activities. Indeed, in order to build a joint innovation–export framework, it is necessary to identify joint innovation–export activities, which require a

1 For the continuation of the study, it was decided to consider only similarities with a degree greater than 0.25; lower similarities are considered less representative.

combination of several common activities and not a simple coupling, as proposed by this similarity matrix.

The next step, therefore, aims to associate, combine and join pairs of common activities (with greater or lesser degrees of similarity) to create emergences and characterize the common innovation–export space. It is, therefore, necessary to exploit and visualize this data differently.

2.1.3.2. *Spatialization of data*

The similarity matrix obtained (see Figure 2.4) highlights the activities that can be considered common to innovation and export. However, group identification is not easy and does not allow for combination as such. It was therefore decided to mobilize data visualization tools.

According to Cleveland (1993), visualization is an essential aspect of data analysis. It reveals the complex structure of data that could not be understood in any other way. It allows unexpected results to be discovered and allows expected conclusions to be questioned. Visualization is, therefore, one of the best ways to explore and try to understand a large amount of data. It is a visual summary of statistical data that makes it easy to see a general trend. However, it is important to keep in mind that a graphical representation is, in essence, a simplification of reality. The multiple parameters of a graphical representation are factors that can, deliberately or not, lead to a distortion of reality. It is therefore important to use appropriate tools and methods in order to obtain the closest representation to reality (Yau 2012).

Data visualization involves the spatialization of data, which implies the transformation of something that is not spatial into something that is. The result is a geometric representation in a small space, usually two or three dimensions, which should allow the detection of trends and relationships invisible in a large database.

The different spatialization methods can be described as follows (Rodrigues *et al.* 2006):

– Modeling: this is the simplest type of spatialization; it consists of associating certain aspects of the data considered with visual properties of geometric forms. For example, thanks to histograms, pie charts, etc.

– Projection: projection corresponds to a display of data through the representation of functional variables. In other words, the position of a data element is defined by a known or implicit mathematical function. Principal component analysis (PCA) is an example of spatialization by projection.

– Reproduction: the positioning of the data comes from the observed phenomenon. It is a question of linking the data to the physical world. For example, the geographical spatialization through maps is an example of reproduction.

– Structuring: this type of spatialization concerns data showing a hierarchical structure and networks. Tools like mind maps, trees or force-directed layout algorithms can be used.

There are many types of data spatialization methods that should be used depending on the data available, the possible correlations between the data and the expected results. It is important to choose the appropriate data spatialization method in order to be able to exploit the data in the most relevant way. For this study, the objective is to characterize a common space between innovation and export activities. This analysis aims to represent similarities, so it was decided to carry out a "structuring" spatialization of the data using Gephi[2] software in order to highlight the links between the activities considered.

Each spatialization method relies on different mathematical algorithms. Within the framework of "structuring" data spatialization methodologies, some algorithms allow a geographical representation of the data, some aim at classifying them and others aim at highlighting divisions or complementarities. This is the case with force-based algorithms. The principle of these algorithms is as follows: each data item is represented by a node (each innovation and export activity is represented by a node). All nodes repel each other, following the principle of magnets. The more dispersed the nodes are, the less they repel each other. Links can be thought of as springs between two nodes (the greater the weight of the link, the stiffer the spring). At each step of the algorithm, the sum of the forces is applied to each node. These nodes move until they reach a stable state. Force-based algorithms position nodes relative to each other. However, the graphs do not always converge to the same final configuration. Therefore, it

2 Gephi is a free software for visualizing and analyzing graphs of any type. This tool allows us to represent, order and arrange structures.

is not possible to read the position of a node per se, and it is necessary to compare its position with others.

Gephi software provides several force-based algorithms, so it was necessary to choose the most suitable algorithm for this analysis. Table 2.2 provides a comparison of these different algorithms.

This comparison highlights some differences between the algorithms considered. Yifan Hu is rather intended to process a large amount of data, which is not the case for this study. This algorithm has therefore been discarded. On the other hand, OpenOrd emphasizes the divisions between the data. For this study, the objective is to highlight similarities. This algorithm was therefore also discarded.

Fruchterman and Rheingold	Yifan Hu	OpenOrd	ForceAtlas/ ForceAtlas 2
Algorithm highlighting the complementarities between the data	Algorithm highlighting complementarities between data; intended for processing large groups of data	Open-source algorithm, putting forward divisions between data	Algorithm highlighting the complementarities between the data

Table 2.2. *Comparison of force-based algorithms available in Gephi software (inspired by Jacomy* et al. *(2014))*

To make a choice between the ForceAtlas and Fruchterman and Rheingold algorithms, it is necessary to go into more detail. These two algorithms are based on an energy model integrating an attraction and repulsion force. They rely, respectively, on a certain formula for the attraction force and a certain formula for the repulsion force, involving the distance d between two nodes. The energy model (a = attraction; r = repulsion) can be defined by considering the exponent assigned to the distance d in the attraction and repulsion force (Noack 2007).

Comparing ForceAtlas2 (an updated version of ForceAtlas) and Fruchterman and Rheingold, their energy models are (1; -1) and (2; -1), respectively. Indeed, the attraction and repulsion forces of the Fruchterman and Rheingold algorithm are defined according to equation [2.1] (Fruchterman and Reingold 1991). The attraction and repulsion forces of the

ForceAltas 2 algorithm are defined according to equation [2.2] (Jacomy *et al.* 2014):

$$\begin{cases} Fa_{F\&R} = \frac{d^2}{k} \\ Fr_{F\&R} = \frac{-k^2}{d} \end{cases} \quad [2.1]$$

$$\begin{cases} Fa_{FA2} = d \\ Fr_{FA2} = \frac{k*C}{d} \end{cases} \quad [2.2]$$

where C and k are constants, and d is the distance between two nodes.

The calculation of *a–r* according to the energy model (*a*; *r*) associated with the algorithm in question provides an additional indication for the choice of the most appropriate algorithm for our study.

According to Noack (2009), a low *a–r* favors the visualization of clusters because it means that the force of attraction depends less on the distance d between two nodes, while the force of repulsion depends more. The *a–r* of the Fruchterman and Rheingold algorithm is 3 (see equation [2.3]), while that for ForceAtlas2 is 2 (see equation [2.4]):

$$a_{F\&R} - r_{F\&R} = 2 - (-1) = 3 \quad [2.3]$$

$$a_{FA2} - r_{FA2} = 1 - (-1) = 2 \quad [2.4]$$

The ForceAtlas2 algorithm, therefore, seems more appropriate for visualizing clusters, which seems relevant for this study. It is, therefore, this algorithm that has been chosen.

A network representation of the data was therefore obtained (see Figure 2.5). Each node represents an innovation or exportation activity. The size of the nodes depends on the number of links they have with other nearby nodes. The more links a node has, the larger its size. The data was then grouped using the "modularity classes" feature. Modularity is often used in optimization methods to detect community structure in networks.

Gephi uses the Leuven modularity calculation method (Blondel *et al.* 2008). It consists of two phases. First, "small" communities are identified by optimizing the modularity in a local way. Second, the nodes of the same community are grouped together, and a new network is built for which the nodes are the communities.

These steps are iteratively repeated until a maximum of modularity is reached. This process naturally leads to the hierarchical decomposition of the network.

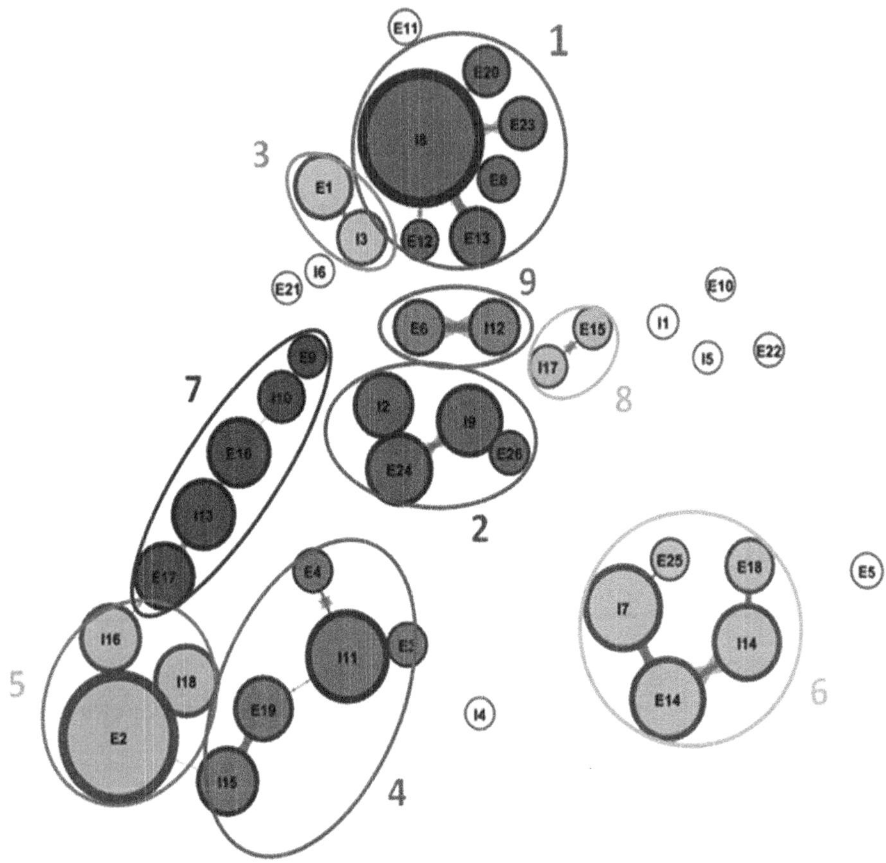

Figure 2.5. *Data spatialization: clustering of common activities. For a color version of the figure, see www.iste.co.uk/enjolras/innovation.zip*

Nine classes of modularity have been identified (see Figure 2.5). The spatialization of activities common to innovation and export thus leads to the identification of nine groups, including activities specific to innovation and activities specific to export. It is, therefore, possible to identify a general theme for each group, according to its composition:

– group 1 gathers the strategic aspects and the prioritization of the company's projects. It can be named strategy;

– group 2 concerns activities related to intellectual assets. It has been named intellectual property;

– group 3 refers to cultural and human aspects. It has been named corporate culture;

– group 4 is composed of activities that concern the customer/user. It can thus be named management of the customer/user relationship;

– group 5 concerns the search for information. It can, therefore, be named monitoring;

– group 6 integrates activities related to the network and skills external to the company. This group has been named networking;

– group 7 concerns knowledge management. It has been named capitalization and exploitation of knowledge;

– group 8 integrates the management of financial resources and project monitoring. It has been named project management;

– group 9 gathers activities related to internal competencies. It can be named human resource management.

Thus, the activities present within a single "modularity class" can be considered to form a joint innovation–export dimension. It is also important to note that only nine activities are not linked to any other (see Figure 2.5). These activities are therefore either purely dedicated to innovation or purely export-oriented. They represent a small proportion of all the activities considered for this analysis. It would therefore seem that the common space between innovation and export is substantial, which confirms the interest in considering innovation and export together.

2.1.3.3. *Towards the identification of joint activities*

In order to propose a framework of joint innovation–export practices, the groups identified through the spatialization of data were decomposed into several joint activities. This decomposition is the result of a combination of the common activities that make up each of the joint dimensions. Thus, the innovation–export common space was identified and characterized through 9 practices (dimensions) and 17 activities, representing our joint assessment framework (see Table 2.3).

Joint dimensions	Common activities included		Joint activities identified
Strategy	I7	Strategic vision	Define a global strategy that simultaneously promotes innovation and export
	E13	Formalization of the strategy	
	I14	Project portfolio	Prioritize projects
	E17	Selection/prioritization	
	E24	Marketing mix	Define the marketing mix strategy
Intellectual property	I17	Intellectual property	Choose and exploit intellectual assets
	E14	Intellectual property	
Company culture	E6	International culture	Encourage autonomy
	I12	Stimulation to innovation	Create the conditions for exchange
Management of the customer/user relationship	I2	User integration	Involve the client/user in the project process
	E23	Product adaptation	
	I9	Customer relations	Manage the customer/user relationship
	E25	Customer relations	
Monitoring	E1	Information acquisition	Search for information
	I3	Monitoring	
Networking	E11	Transport	Mobilize weak networks (external organizations, service providers, etc.)
	E7	Communication/translation	
	E19	Management of suppliers	Manage strong networks (partnerships, suppliers, distributors, etc.)
	E22	Strategy of distribution	
	E12	Partnerships	
	I8	Networking	

<table>
<tr><th>Joint dimensions</th><th colspan="2">Common activities included</th><th>Joint activities identified</th></tr>
<tr><td rowspan="3">Capitalization and exploitation of knowledge</td><td>I18</td><td>Capitalization of knowledge</td><td rowspan="3">Store knowledge
Share and use knowledge</td></tr>
<tr><td>E2</td><td>Capitalization and sharing</td></tr>
<tr><td>I16</td><td>Continuous improvement</td></tr>
<tr><td rowspan="5">Project management</td><td>E16</td><td>Project process management</td><td rowspan="2">Plan projects</td></tr>
<tr><td>I13</td><td>Project monitoring</td></tr>
<tr><td>E15</td><td>Dedicated resources</td><td rowspan="3">Allocate material and financial resources</td></tr>
<tr><td>I10</td><td>Financial agility</td></tr>
<tr><td>E8</td><td>Search of funding</td></tr>
<tr><td rowspan="5">Human resource management</td><td>E4</td><td>Technical and commercial skills</td><td rowspan="3">Manage skills (training, recruitment, etc.)</td></tr>
<tr><td>E3</td><td>Linguistic skills</td></tr>
<tr><td>I11</td><td>Skills management</td></tr>
<tr><td>E18</td><td>Organization of responsibilities</td><td rowspan="2">Mobilize and allocate human resources (organization of tasks and responsibilities)</td></tr>
<tr><td>I15</td><td>Organization of tasks</td></tr>
</table>

Table 2.3. *Construction of the joint reference system: combination of joint innovation–export activities*

2.2. What about the field?

Although there is a great deal of research on the innovation–export nexus, there is little work on the operational translation of this nexus and thus few joint frames of reference. Existing research that mentions the notion of a joint reference framework refers to frameworks for the analysis of the innovation–export link. As an example, Chen *et al.* (2018) propose a mutualized model to estimate the direct and indirect effects of exporting on company innovation. In the same vein, Gkypali *et al.* (2018) propose a theoretical framework that includes absorptive capacity, export activity, openness to innovation and innovation performance and studies the mutual effects of these factors. These frameworks are thus primarily means of analyzing the innovation–export relationship and not a representation of this relationship as such.

No.	Potential synergies	Items discussed in the interview
(1)	Definition of a global strategy and prioritization of of projects	Definition of strategy, prioritization of prioritization, marketing mix strategy, etc.
(2)	Management and exploitation of intellectual property	Choice of intellectual property tools, management of intellectual property, exploitation of intellectual property assets
(3)	Dissemination of the corporate culture	Encouraging autonomy, sharing information and experiences
(4)	Taking the customer into account	Customer relationship management, involvement of customers/users in the process project process
(5)	Acquisition of information and knowledge	Information research: technological and commercial watch
(6)	Mobilization of external skills	Networking, mobilization of external skills, working with partners (suppliers, distributors, etc.)
(7)	Capitalization and sharing of knowledge	Information storage, sharing and exploitation of knowledge
(8)	Allocation of financial resources and monitoring of projects	Material resource allocation, project coordination/planning
(9)	Human resource allocation and internal skills management	Affecting human resources (tasks and responsibilities), skills management

Table 2.4. *Interview grid from the joint innovation–export practice benchmark*

By proposing a joint innovation–export practice benchmark (see section 2.1.3.3), we fill this gap. This reference framework allows us to understand how the company manages joint innovation–export activities by looking at the internal practices/routines of companies. However, this reference framework is based on theoretical foundations that must be confronted with the reality of the business world in order to attest to the veracity and relevance of the proposed reference framework. Through 11 semi-directive interviews conducted with innovative and exporting French SMEs, various illustrative examples of synergy effects between innovation and export were identified and put into perspective with regard to the proposed joint reference framework.

2.2.1. *Presentation of the consulted companies and method*

The objective of this empirical study, based on a cross-case analysis, was to identify illustrative examples of synergy effects between innovation and export activities implemented within companies. The 11 cases studied are presented in Table 2.5. In constructing this sample, care was taken to balance the sizes of the companies represented as well as the differences in terms of export turnover. However, no selection was made in terms of business sector. Instead, we took into account firms with high-, medium- and low-technology activities (Hatzichronoglou 1997).

Case	Business sector	Size (OECD)	Sales turnover in exports
A	Scientific optical equipment	Small	70%
B	Welding equipment	Small	30%
C	Scientific instruments	Micro	50%
D	Agricultural machinery	Average	6%
E	Food industry	Micro	4%
F	Electronics, automatics	Small	1%
G	Thermoplastic materials	Small	15%
H	Biotechnology	Micro	5%
I	Telecommunication equipment	Micro	95%
J	Plastic materials	Small	40%
K	Food industry	Medium	5%

Table 2.5. *Sample of companies consulted*

The companies were selected according to different criteria. First, the company needed to be an SME according to the European Commission's definition (European Commission 2016c): less than 250 employees and a turnover of less than €50 million. We thus excluded start-ups from our sample due to their specificities in terms of internal organization. Second, the company needed to be an exporting SME: export sales of over 1%. Third, we only took into account companies for which we could have a direct relationship with the manager in order to keep a standard data collection process.

These interviews consisted of questioning company managers about their innovation and export practices and took place in several stages:

– the preparation phase: a first contact was established with the company in order to inform the manager of our approach. Following this first contact, a meeting was scheduled. At the same time, some information about the company was collected in order to prepare the interview (industry, export turnover, size of the company, products, etc.);

– the interview: each interview lasted between one and two hours. After a brief presentation of the context of our study, the interview with the manager allowed us to review all the joint practices of the benchmark. The objective was to clearly identify the way the company managed innovation and implementation on a daily basis, using examples and factual evidence to illustrate this (observable phenomena);

– the results: following the interview, a summary report was written and sent by e-mail to the company. This report contained a summary of the issues discussed during the interview.

Then, using a cross-case study approach, the content of each interview was qualitatively analyzed practice by practice in order to identify some examples (or counter-examples) of synergistic effects between innovation and exporting. Based on our repository of joint practices, we identified observable phenomena that describe the internal practices of companies regarding their innovation and export activities. From the list of observable phenomena of each company, it was possible to identify synergistic effects in different ways:

– whether an observable phenomenon is common to both innovation and export;

– whether an observable phenomenon associated with the company's export activities is in fact a facilitator of innovation;

– whether an observable phenomenon dedicated to the company's innovation activities is also a facilitator of export.

The results of this cross-analysis highlight field observations that confirm or refute the relevance of the joint practices identified in the proposed framework. They also highlight key points to be considered as strategic to promote synergies between innovation and export.

2.2.2. *Highlighting synergies*

2.2.2.1. *The strategy*

The analysis of the cross-case studies has made it possible to identify interesting observations concerning the definition of the strategy of the innovative and exporting companies in the panel. The main conclusion concerns the coupling of innovation and international development strategies. It seems particularly relevant to move towards a vision in terms of a "product–market pair" integrating a specific strategic differentiation. This product–market vision is strongly linked to the notion of the marketing mix within the SMEs interviewed. Thus, for each product–market pair, the company must be able to define common strategies for four main criteria.

First of all, a specific strategy must be built for the product according to the targeted market: for example, company A has chosen to position itself on a strong differentiation strategy for its product–market couple. It sells components for scientific instrumentation machines requiring extreme precision. The joint innovation–export strategy of company A results in a systematic adaptation of the product–market couple for each customer. This is due to the fact that company A is positioned in a niche market, gathering very diverse demands and obliging it to supply "tailor-made" products all over the world. Another example of this product–market adaptation is offered by company B, which modifies the characteristics of its products according to the target market. Company B's products are tools for processing metal parts. The main reason for these adaptations is to comply with current standards and regulations, which vary from country to country. In addition, the specific modes and conditions of use of the products can also vary, which means that company B is obliged to improve certain functionalities of these products, in particular, to resist extreme climatic conditions.

On the other hand, a pricing strategy must be anticipated. Exporting usually implies additional costs for the product compared to the domestic market. In some cases, this makes the company less competitive in its future market. The company must therefore be able to position its price offer in relation to its competitors and therefore differentiate it according to the target markets. This is the current problem of company C, a French high-tech SME that is considering a future development in the United States.

The difficulty in finding the necessary information to position the company in relation to its foreign competitors is a real obstacle to international development, and it is essential to anticipate these problems.

Then, the communication strategy around the product must be different. This theme came up in every interview we conducted: Updating the website in multiple languages? What information should be highlighted according to the target market? Do the existing communication documents reflect the positioning chosen by the company?

Finally, the distribution strategy is the last element of the marketing mix to anticipate. Depending on the target market, the company must differentiate its distribution channels and methods. The notion of product–market coupling has thus become omnipresent within company D since it launched a development in Latin America. The company sells agricultural machinery worldwide through a robust export process but is currently experiencing difficulties in penetrating the Brazilian market due to the country's specific international trade policy. Exports, the company's preferred method of internationalization, have not been possible. The company is therefore considering an external growth strategy specifically for this market.

Thus, the differentiation of the product–market pair can take different forms, but it seems to be a strategic element adopted by companies, allowing them to have a prospective vision of their joint development in terms of innovation and export.

2.2.2.2. *Management of the network*

While networking is a powerful driver of innovative capacity (Eggers *et al.* 2018), it is also a major facilitator of international development for SMEs (Montoro-Sanchez *et al.* 2018). The synergistic effects of networks are reflected in the company's ability to recreate a prolific ecosystem in a new market so as to identify and exploit opportunities. Thus, company D illustrates the importance of the ecosystem for both innovation and international business development. This company has built its innovation model on close collaboration with its suppliers. The challenge for this company's international development is to be able to rebuild an equivalent ecosystem abroad, in order to "export its competitive advantage".

The identification of collaboration opportunities plays an essential role, and company C offers a very interesting illustrative case study. This company relies on a network of partners who act as customers, innovation partners and prescribers: researchers (university or private) using their scientific instrumentation tools. Company C relies on the network of these partners to reach a wider audience (the scientific community) and identify original ways to improve products.

Finally, the term "hunting in a pack" is a recurrent element in the interviews, particularly in the case of smaller companies. It is a way of pooling the costs and risks of exporting by joining forces with partners with similar ambitions. Company E sells agri-food products in several Asian countries by participating in a network of agri-food companies grouped under the "made in France" label.

2.2.2.3. *Knowledge management and organization of internal processes*

While the management of the company's network opens up external perspectives, practices related to its internal organization are also redundant in the interviews.

As explained in Chapter 1 (see section 1.2.3.2), innovation and exporting are considered "denaturing" activities. This notion of "denaturing" appears systematically in the interviews conducted. It is expressed in several ways.

First, through the issue of learning: innovation and exporting create change within the company. To manage this change, the company must become a learning organization to adapt to it. Company E provides a good example of a learning process. This young exporting company, in the IT and automation sector, has started its international development towards countries that are geographically and culturally close. Today, it plans to position itself in the United States, but it is facing major administrative difficulties. It, therefore, plans to implement a step-by-step learning process, initially targeting Quebec (Canada) in order to familiarize itself with North American formalities and the associated culture, but in a familiar language. In addition, it is the only company on the panel to have set up a shared and collaborative knowledge management platform, which is unusual for this type of small company.

Company F is following the same direction, as it is engaged in a business change from a subcontractor in the plastics industry to a manufacturer in its own right. To do this, it is using the launch of an ISO-9001 certification process to strengthen its skills and structure its internal processes.

Finally, companies G and H face the same development problem. They are both making the transition from international start-ups to high-growth SMEs. This transition requires them to formalize their processes in order to continue their development and move to a multi-site deployment. For example, company G is testing a remote collaboration tool to move from a start-up's style of informal and continuous communication to organized and shared communication, both geographically and temporally. Similarly, company H inaugurates a project management tool to facilitate its internal organization and the distribution of tasks between employees working remotely. Thus, each at its own scale, companies E, F, G and H are transforming themselves into learning organizations to manage the common challenges of international development and innovation.

2.2.2.4. *Client management and information gathering*

During the interviews, the themes of customer relationship management and information gathering were regularly discussed. Three companies emphasized the importance of combining commercial and technical skills, both in terms of customer relations, to be able to inform and understand them, and in terms of competitive and technological intelligence.

Companies C and D particularly emphasized their desire to recruit and train employees who are comfortable with both the technical operation of the product and the way it is sold. Indeed, company C insists on this point, as it is a strategic vector of information concerning the future development of the product. Contacts with customers and a good understanding of their needs are a source of innovation and competitive advantage in international and national markets.

Company D, on the other hand, brings this issue closer to after-sales service. Because of its business, company D must maintain close relations with its customers to train them and maintain their equipment. This regular contact with customers is also a way to bring out valuable information.

Finally, company J, an international SME that sells delineation products for public spaces, translates this commercial/technical coupling by considering that the key point of an innovation and export strategy is the search for valuable and rare information about the customer: identifying prospects that can afford to pay and targeting product developments to which these prospects do not have access. For this company, it is essential to make the link between commercial and technological intelligence in the different markets (and therefore in several languages) for better consistency.

2.2.2.5. *Corporate culture and openness*

The elements put forward by the companies concern strategic, prospective, organizational and managerial aspects. However, the fertile ground for all of these elements lies in the culture and openness that the company disseminates to its employees. The terms "common dynamics", "sense of belonging", "commitment" and "diversity" seem to be the watchwords of the companies interviewed. Thus, it seems essential to create the right conditions to support both the innovation and export dynamics of the company. For company K, this is fundamental and translates into the involvement of the entire company in the international and innovative process. Company K is a small- and medium-sized company in the agri-food sector, which has been exporting for many years. This company regularly develops new products for its national and/or international markets and has developed an internal culture of experimentation. In general, exports start with small volumes. However, from a production efficiency point of view, there is not necessarily an internal interest in small volumes. This leads to additional handling and slows down production. It also leads to regular packaging changes and the associated constraints. These changes must be internally accepted to create a virtuous loop so that everyone feels part of this dynamic. Company C also manages these cultural aspects, but with a view to diversity and openness, by encouraging exchanges and experiences. Thus, international collaborators are regularly integrated into the team to bring new points of view and enrich and energize collaborations.

2.2.2.6. *The specific issue of intellectual property management*

This cross-sectional approach brought to light various elements of empirical responses concerning the joint vision of innovation and exporting. Eight of the nine joint practices in the reference framework were addressed during the interviews, although some were merged in the following restitution:

– strategy (1);

– network (6);

– knowledge management (7), human resources (9), project management (8);

– customer relations (4) and monitoring (5);

– corporate culture (3).

The last joint practice to be discussed concerns the management of intellectual property (IP) (2). This theme has given rise to various observations within companies, reflecting different positions. First of all, the first scenario presents IP as a secondary element for the company. It does not feel concerned. This is particularly the case for company F. However, this can be explained by the industry in which it operates, requiring a particular management of IP: electronics and information technology. The second case concerns companies that manage their P under particular constraints and do the minimum. They consider this issue only as a means of protection but without any other added value. The third and last case is where companies manage their IP as intangible assets. They exploit their property titles (resale of patents or licensing, for example) but consider mainly the financial aspect of IP and not its strategic aspect. This is particularly the case for company H. However, IP can be a very powerful tool for improving the company's image with the customer and can also be a tool for technological and competitive positioning. Only companies K and E take this dimension slightly into account by positioning their brand in the line of "made in France", an important valuation argument in the agri-food sector.

Thus, the management of intellectual property is considered by SMEs more as an obligatory constraint or a potential source of revenue rather than as a strategic tool for a common vision of innovation and international development. It would seem that this practice is more widespread in the context of large companies.

2.2.3. *Discussions*

This research work is based on the comparison of a theoretical model of the relationship between innovation and exporting with the reality of the SME world. By highlighting the results of a cross-analysis based on case studies, the conclusions highlight illustrative cases of synergistic effects between innovation and export activities put into practice within companies.

Five dimensions were addressed:

– the ability to build a joint innovation–export strategy through a vision of the product and the market as an inseparable couple;

– the (re)creation of an effective ecosystem/network leading to the identification of opportunities;

– managing change through the progressive structuring of internal processes – becoming a learning organization;

– the coupling of technical and commercial skills to improve the relationship with the customer and to favor the collection of information;

– the need to create the right conditions for openness and involvement through a strong corporate culture.

Thus, the main conclusion of this research work is that a joint vision of innovation and export activities within companies seems relevant, according to the results of our sample. Eight of the nine common dimensions of our joint practice framework have given rise to interesting illustrative examples. However, the issue of IP leads to more differentiated findings, but one that remains related to the difficulties and reluctance of SMEs to use IP protection tools in general (Hanel 2006; Hughes and Mina 2010; Thomä and Bizer 2013).

Thus, from both a theoretical and managerial point of view, it seems relevant to consider these synergies between innovation and export activities as drivers of SME development and growth. Seeking to exploit these synergistic effects as a priority contributes to reducing the effort associated with the creation of an innovation–export virtuous circle within SMEs. The identification and characterization of these synergies, therefore, offer avenues to explore in order to contribute to the proposal of a support system for SMEs that encourages companies to act on joint practices that they should mobilize as a priority to simultaneously improve their innovation and export performance.

The proposed joint innovation–export practice framework is, therefore, the basis for the main contribution of this research work. It is, in fact, the key element of a system that aims to operationalize the relationship between innovation and export through the proposal of a support tool for SMEs. This tool, called "PE2I" (Potential Innovation and Export Index), acts as a strategic decision-making tool. It is based on a multi-criteria analysis methodology to model the innovation–export relationship through the complexity paradigm and to support the decision-making process through a joint evaluation of the innovation and export capabilities of SMEs.

PART 2

PE2I, or How to Model Synergies

3

Design of a Joint Diagnosis Dedicated to SMEs: The PE2I

The objective of this chapter is to describe the design process of the PE2I (Potential Innovation and Export Index), as well as its operational development. This decision support tool is intended to evaluate SMEs' innovation and export capabilities by measuring the maturity of joint innovation–export activities carried out within companies.

Thus, this tool makes it possible to propose a diagnosis of a company's situation at a given moment: it identifies the company's strengths and weaknesses and gives an indication of its potential field of predilection (innovation and/or export). However, this tool also makes it possible to suggest ways of improving the company's development strategy. Does the company want to promote its export development? Then, the tool will identify the main levers to achieve this objective. On the contrary, does the company want to focus more significantly on innovation? The tool will then propose potentially different levers of action. Does the company want to implement a joint innovation–export improvement strategy? Here again, adapted action levers will be identified.

3.1. The methodological framework

The PE2I is the result of the merger of the Potential Innovation Index (PII), which characterizes a framework of practices specific to innovation, and the Potential Export Index (PEI), which represents the dimensions specific to export, as described in Chapter 2 of this book. The PE2I thus characterizes the common innovation–export space through a reference framework of joint practices (see Figure 3.1). Because it is based on existing and compatible frames of reference (the PII and the PEI), it is built on a similar methodological basis and is therefore in line with the work carried out in this direction.

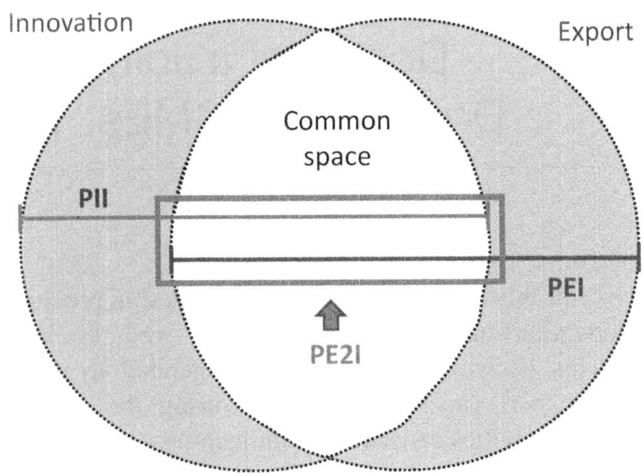

Figure 3.1. *Scope of PE2I. For a color version of the figure, see www.iste.co.uk/enjolras/innovation.zip*

3.1.1. *The methodological background*

The methodological basis used is in line with the research work carried out by the ERPI laboratory at the University of Lorraine, which has developed a process for designing multi-criteria decision support tools based on the metrology of internal processes in companies. Initiated with the design of the Potential Innovation Index (PII), this methodology is based on three blocks.

The first block consists of creating an evaluation framework system. To do this, best internal practices from the literature are identified and validated both theoretically and empirically. These practices are then structured according to three hierarchical levels: each identified practice is divided into activities, which are themselves characterized in the form of observable phenomena. The last step consists of transforming this structure into an evaluation framework. To do this, it is necessary to introduce the notion of indicators. Each activity in the framework is then characterized through different maturity levels that describe a situation with which the company being evaluated can identify. To do this, the observable phenomena associated with it are organized to form an evaluation grid that measures the level of mastery of the activity in question. Each level of this grid is therefore considered as an indicator of the evaluation framework system.

The second block concerns the construction of a mathematical evaluation model. This model is based on the aggregation of the evaluations of each practice, thus allowing the calculation of a score called "global index". The framework of practices previously constructed is therefore weighted according to the importance or contribution of each of them to the targeted result. Thus, in the case of the PII, the weighting constructed highlights the innovation practices with the greatest importance, and therefore the greatest impact on the company's innovation capability. This weighting step is a way to propose a framework that is closer to reality. On the basis of the weighted framework, it is then possible to calculate a global index translating, in the case of the PII, the general innovation capability of the company. This global index represents a score that allows the company to be classified in a category that reflects a certain attitude towards innovation.

Finally, the third block concerns the generation of personalized recommendations allowing the company to identify potential improvement paths. These recommendations are identified on the basis of the company's initial profile (the result of its assessment) and take into account the weighting of each practice. Thus, the recommendation system favors actions on the most influential practices without systematically trying to act on the weakest points. In this way, the effort associated with the company's improvement is optimized and personalized.

Evaluation framework	**Evaluation model**	**System of recommendations**
Establishing the company's maturity profile	Weighting and characterization of the evaluation model using multi-criteria tools	Identifying customized improvement paths

Table 3.1. *Methodological steps*

3.1.2. *The methodological tools used*

The methodological tools supporting this process are, on the one hand, the maturity grids that make it possible to measure the degree of mastery of each activity. We then move from a framework of practices to an evaluation system assessing the maturity of these practices, where the maturity grids act as measurement indicators. On the other hand, multi-criteria analysis methods allow the design of the mathematical evaluation model and the creation of a representative global index. These methods make it possible to translate the complexity of the model and to aggregate its various components.

3.1.2.1. *Maturity grids*

Maturity grids are regularly used to measure the internal practices of organizations (Lianying *et al.* 2012; Wendler 2012; Antunes *et al.* 2014). According to Andersen and Jessen (2003), the maturity in an organization can be defined as the maximum degree of development, that is, the optimal working conditions to achieve the objectives. Maturity grids, therefore, describe in a progressive and gradual way the steps needed to reach a maximum level of development regarding a given activity. They can be represented in the form of a staircase, the steps of which must be climbed in order to gradually reach the maximum level of development (see Figure 3.2).

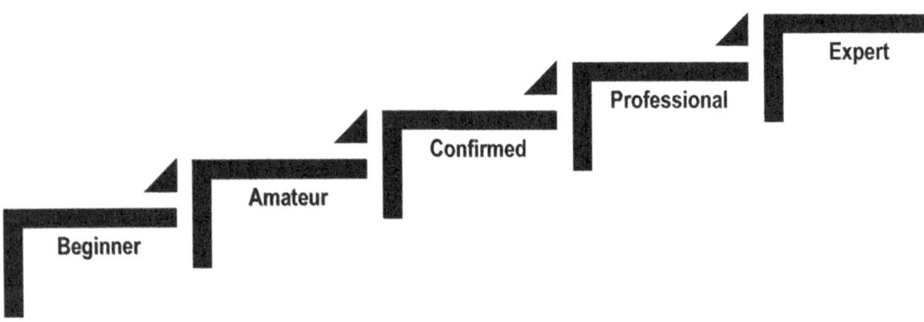

Figure 3.2. *Example of a graphical representation of a maturity grid*

The main benefits of the maturity grid are as follows:

– Adaptability: the maturity grid can be built in different configurations to better adapt to the requirements of the process to be measured.

– Clarity: the maturity grids are formulated using multiple choice questions that represent levels of performance/mastery. The creation of these grids requires the formulation of descriptive texts corresponding to each level of the grid in question. These texts facilitate the understanding of the grid and ensure a certain objectivity during the evaluation.

– Transparency: the ascending progression of the maturity grids makes it possible to know all the steps necessary to reach the maximum level. This allows the company to identify short- and medium-term progression objectives, according to its assessment. It can then define an improvement strategy.

3.1.2.2. *Multi-criteria analysis methods*

Since the 1980s, the primary role of multi-criteria analysis has evolved from a multi-objective optimization process to a way of providing decision support to decision-makers. Through the development of multi-criteria decision-making systems (MCDMS), it is now possible to reflect the decision maker's choice mechanism and the systemic nature of the decision process instead of solving well-structured problems based on assumptions (Korhonen *et al.* 1992). MCDMS provide support to decision-makers by modeling and structuring a coherent picture of complex decision problems they face (Kurka and Blackwood 2013). Thus, in the context of our study, these tools are powerful levers to support SMEs in their decision-making processes so that they can manage the complexity associated with managing "denaturing" activities such as innovation and export.

There are many methods of multi-criteria analysis. Among the most well-known, MAUT (Multi-Attribute Utility Theory) consists of calculating a utility function for each criterion studied (Sanayei *et al.* 2008; Kim and Song 2009); AHP (Analytic Hierarchy Process) decomposes the problem into a hierarchical structure and allows the criteria to be weighted (Saaty and Kearns 1985); Promethee (Preference Ranking Organization Method for Enrichment Evaluations) compares actions two by two in order to deduce a list of preferences (Albadvi *et al.* 2007; Ishizaka and Nemery 2011; Abedi *et al.* 2012); and finally, sorting methods classify actions into predefined categories (Zopounidis and Doumpos 2002; Nemery and Lamboray 2008).

The choice of which method to use depends on the type of problem to be solved. Therefore, these methodologies can be classified into different categories (Galvez 2015):

– Descriptive methods: they seek either to determine the variables representative of the problem (Yam *et al.* 2004; Forsman 2011; Martínez-Román *et al.* 2011; Liu *et al.* 2012) or to propose a performance profile by evaluating each criterion individually. The latter are a criterion-by-criterion analysis tool; they present incompatibility problems when we wish to propose an overall analysis (Nemery 2009). These descriptive methods were therefore not used in this research, as they do not meet our need for a simultaneous and global multi-criteria evaluation.

– Ranking methods: the objective of these methods is to prioritize alternatives by calculating a global aggregated index. They are based on the principle of total or partial aggregation. Total aggregation means considering that the score attributed to one action does not depend on the others. Partial aggregation, on the contrary, results in a relative score, taking into account the comparison of actions between them. Depending on the aggregation method chosen, a compensation phenomenon may also occur. This occurs when a high performance on one criterion hides a deficient performance on another (Guitouni and Martel 1998; Cinelli *et al.* 2014). These ranking methods were used in Block 1 of the index design process through the weighting of practices. Specifically, the AHP method was used.

– Sorting methods: like ranking methods, sorting methods allow the calculation of a global index. But this time, this index does not lead to a prioritization of the alternatives but to a classification of these alternatives within predefined categories. The use of these sorting methods corresponds to Block 2 of the process presented earlier (see section 3.1.1), allowing the calculation of an overall score following the evaluation of the company. More specifically, the FlowSort method was used.

3.1.3. *PII and PEI as a basis for development*

The PII and PEI frameworks, which are the basis of this research work, represent the methodological basis of the future joint PE2I index. They are based on the three development blocks previously defined (see section 3.1.1) and mobilize the multi-criteria analysis methods and maturity grids (see Figure 3.3). This section aims to detail their structure and operating principle in order to integrate them as pillars of the PE2I design process.

Both the PII and the PEI are based on a hierarchical assessment framework with three levels of aggregation: practices, activities and observable phenomena, as outlined in Chapter 2. This hierarchical structure should therefore also be followed by the joint practices framework of the PE2I.

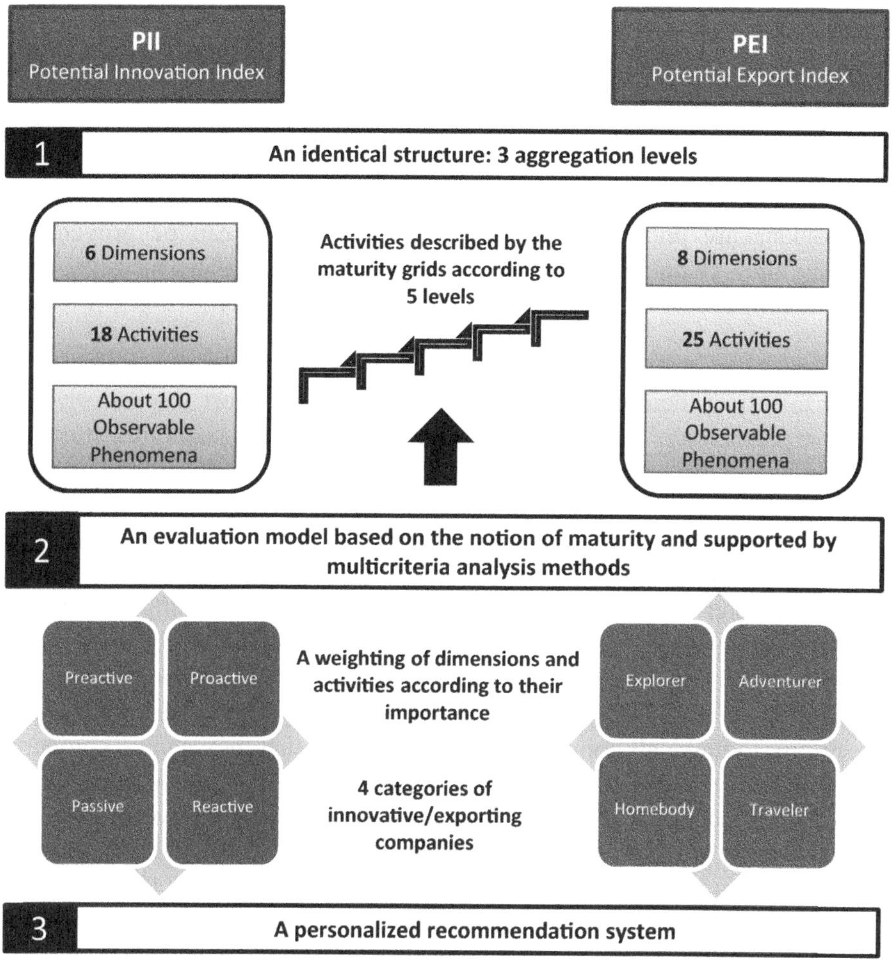

Figure 3.3. *The common structure of the PII and the PEI*

In order to move from a framework of practices to an evaluation model, each activity (respectively innovation and export) of the PII and PEI has been described through maturity grids. They allow the evaluation of the degree of maturity of the company regarding a specific activity and are based on descriptive texts that allow the identification of the situation that best corresponds to the company. These descriptive texts highlight different observable phenomena, which can be defined as tangible and verifiable evidence that a practice is routinely carried out within the company (e.g. presence of a specific digital tool, formalized procedures for data exploitation and meeting minutes). These observable phenomena act as indicators for evaluating the practice. The use of observable phenomena also limits subjectivity in the evaluation of the company. Each level in the maturity grids is descriptive and can be interpreted differently by different people. Levels based on tangible, verifiable evidence reduce this interpretability and make the diagnosis more objective. If these observable phenomena are present in the company and if they can be proven, the practice they characterize can be considered mastered. The maturity grids will, therefore, also be used within the framework of PE2I.

Within the evaluation model, practices and activities are weighted in order to reflect their impact on the innovation and export respectively in a more realistic way. These weights were defined on the basis of a literature review and consultations with experts using the AHP multi-criteria analysis method. The AHP methodology is based on the principle of pairwise comparison on the basis of experts' opinions. It results in a weighting of the criteria using the Saaty scale, which measures the preference of the decision-maker for one criterion over another, and by assigning a numerical value to the level of preference. The scale is progressive: a value of 1 means that the two criteria are "equally important", and a 9 means that one criterion is "extremely more important" than the other (Saaty 1980). The objective is, therefore, to make all combinations of criteria so that they can be compared with each other. These comparisons were submitted to innovation and export experts, respectively. The export experts were approached through an online questionnaire in which each expert had to follow the AHP methodology and make the comparisons one by one in order to assess the importance of each practice in the companies' export activities. The eight responses obtained were checked for consistency and averaged across all consistent responses to propose a consensus set of export-oriented weights (Enjolras 2016). The innovation weighting was based on preliminary research by Galvez (2015), using interviews with researchers and institutions specializing in innovation in the form of a focus group. This allowed for an assessment of the importance of each practice for the innovation activities of the companies.

For both innovation and export, the PII and PEI indexes make it possible to calculate an aggregated score based on the evaluation of a company, making it possible to identify its behavior, respectively in terms of innovation and export, by classifying them in a specific category.

Thus, the PII is based on four categories describing the innovation profile of companies:

– passive companies;

– reactive companies;

– preactive companies;

– proactive companies.

They show the innovation dynamics of companies and their attitude towards novelty and are constructed in a gradual way in terms of involvement in innovation. Thus, passive companies have a very low innovation capability and are mainly oriented towards a dynamic of adaptation. Proactive companies have a long-term vision, adopting a proactive strategy and an anticipatory attitude (Godet 1997).

Similarly, the categories describing the export profile are as follows:

– homebodies: companies that export on a very irregular basis, generally by opportunity. They target markets that are close (culturally and geographically) in order to limit risks;

– travelers: companies exporting regularly, but limited to close and reassuring countries;

– explorers: companies for which export sales represent a significant part of their turnover. They export regularly and intensively to easily accessible countries and also target more distant countries;

– adventurers: companies for which exporting is second nature. Geographical and cultural distance is not a problem. They export continuously and intensively to markets that are considered difficult to access.

To perform this aggregation step and arrive at a global index, the FlowSort multi-criteria analysis method was chosen. This method is a direct extension of the Promethee method, which is based on a flow calculation.

A special feature of FlowSort is that, unlike Electre-Tri, the most widely used sorting method (Ishizaka and Nemery 2013), the assignment of an evaluation to a category depends on an overall comparison with all category boundary profiles simultaneously. Indeed, FlowSort addresses a sorting problem through a ranking method that is therefore applied to all data, consisting of both evaluations and reference profiles. The category attribution will then be deduced from the relative position of the evaluation with respect to the reference profiles in the obtained ranking (Nemery and Lamboray 2008). FlowSort therefore proposes a global approach by proposing a comparison with all the limit profiles and is based on a well-known ranking methodology: Promethee.

Finally, the PII and PEI, respectively, allow the generation of personalized recommendations, allowing the identification of priority improvement paths for companies. These recommendations are based on the company's initial profile and, based on the assessments obtained via the maturity grids, identify the activities on which to take priority action, taking into account their weighting (and therefore their potential impact on the final index).

3.2. The construction of the PE2I

Based on the above, this section presents the steps in the construction of the PE2I, an assessment tool measuring the innovation and export capabilities of SMEs, highlighting the synergies between these two activities as a potential driver of development.

Its methodological foundations are based on the following three steps: creation of a joint innovation–export maturity profile, development of an evaluation model and design of a personalized recommendation system.

3.2.1. *Step 1: create a maturity profile*

The first step of the PE2I assessment is to establish the company's profile by measuring the degree of maturity of its internal processes regarding innovation and export.

To do this, the assessment is based on a reference framework of 17 maturity grids, representing the 17 joint activities of the innovation–export reference framework (see Table 3.3).

In the case of PE2I, the maturity grids describe five progressive levels (see Table 3.2). In an interview with the SME's manager, a score between 1 and 5 is assigned to each of the 17 maturity grids. If the company does not correctly master the activity assessed, its score will be 1 (beginner level) or 2 (amateur level). However, if the company shows a good mastery of the activity, its score will be 4 (confirmed level) or 5 (expert level).

Level 1 beginner	Level 2 amateur	Level 3 intermediate	Level 4 confirmed	Level 5 expert
Knowledge is not shared	Knowledge is shared informally and spontaneously	Experts are identified within the company for their particular knowledge. They are regularly consulted if necessary	A procedure for disseminating and sharing information is in place (inter-service meetings, experience sharing, mailing, training, etc.)	Digital tools allow information to be shared and used on a daily basis, at any time and in any place. Priority or critical information is identified, easily accessible and taken into account according to its impact on the company's strategy. Data exploitation procedures are implemented

Table 3.2. *Example of a "knowledge sharing and exploitation" practice maturity grid*

On the basis of the 17 scores obtained, an aggregation based on the average is carried out in order to visualize an overall profile of the enterprise according to the nine joint innovation–export practices of the reference framework (see Figure 3.4). It is then possible to visualize the strengths and weaknesses of the company and to establish a detailed profile of the way in which it conducts joint innovation and export activities.

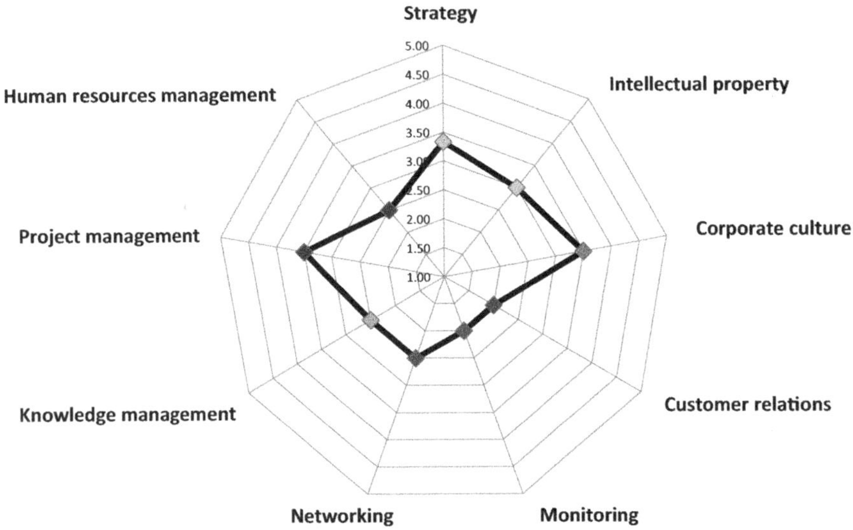

Figure 3.4. *Representation of a company's profile. For a color version of the figure, see www.iste.co.uk/enjolras/innovation.zip*

3.2.2. *Step 2: weighting and characterization of the evaluation model using multi-criteria analysis tools*

The second step in the design of this decision-making tool is to aggregate the company's maturity scores into a Potential Export and Innovation Index (PE2I). This aggregation step is based on a combination of two multi-criteria analysis methodologies: AHP (Saaty 1980) and FlowSort (Nemery and Lamboray 2007). These two methodologies make it possible to construct a global vision of a company's innovation and export capabilities, as well as its potential predisposition to innovation or exporting (see Figure 3.5).

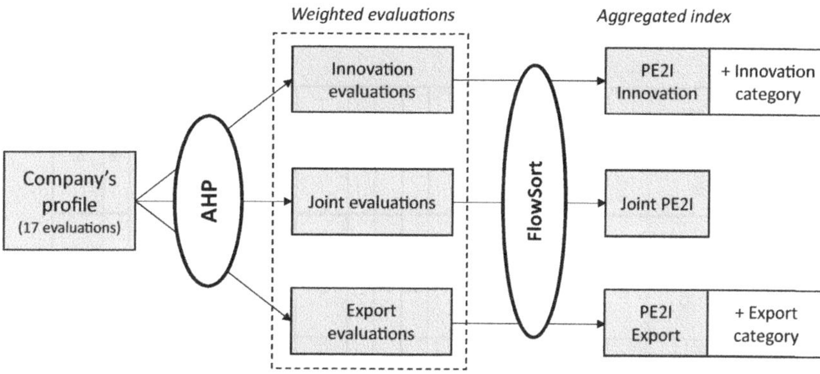

Figure 3.5. *Aggregation steps*

3.2.2.1. *The weighting of activities*

The first step is to propose a weighting of the joint practices according to their importance in terms of both innovation and exports. As indicated earlier (see section 3.1.3), certain practices have a greater or lesser influence on the innovation capability of companies. These same practices also have varying degrees of importance in the assessment of export capability. On the basis of this hypothesis, a differentiated weighting of the practices in the joint reference framework allows for a more in-depth diagnosis by identifying a potential predisposition to innovation or export. The AHP methodology was therefore used.

For operational reasons, it was decided that the activities that make up a single practice were equivalent in terms of importance: they are equally weighted. The AHP methodology was therefore applied only to the first level of aggregation (the nine joint practices). Based on the weights used in the respective mathematical models of the PII and PEI, a joint weight was also constructed, based on the average of the other two (see Table 3.3). The proposal of three different weights avoids an offsetting effect related to an average calculation. The joint weighting gives an overall view of the relative importance of each practice in the benchmark, but the export- and innovation-oriented weightings add nuance by highlighting a potential predisposition of companies either to innovation or to exporting. For example, it appears that the joint practice "knowledge management" has a medium impact on joint innovation–export capability (joint weighting of 12%). But on closer inspection, it appears that its impact is, in fact, much greater on innovation (19%) than on export (5%).

Joint practices	[A] Innovation-oriented weighting	[C]= ([A]+[B])/2 Joint Innovation/ Export weighting	[B] Export-oriented weighting	Joint activities	[D] Weighting of joint activities	[E] = [C]*[D] Relative joint weighting
Strategy	12%	15%	17%	Defining a global strategy that simultaneously promotes innovation and export	33%	5%
				Prioritizing projects	33%	5%
				Defining the marketing mix strategy	33%	5%
Intellectual property	8%	7%	7%	Choosing and exploiting intellectual assets protection	100%	7%
Corporate culture	4%	8%	12%	Encouraging autonomy	50%	4%
				Creating conditions for interaction	50%	4%
Customer relations	14%	13%	12%	Managing the customer/user relationship	50%	6%
				Involve the client/user in the project process	50%	6%
Monitoring	9%	7%	5%	Seeking information	100%	7%
Networking	14%	14%	13%	Mobilizing weak networks (external organizations, service providers)	50%	7%
				Managing strong networks (partners, suppliers, etc.)	50%	7%
Knowledge management	19%	12%	5%	Storing knowledge	50%	6%
				Sharing and using knowledge	50%	6%
Project management	5%	9%	14%	Assigning material and financial resources	50%	5%
				Planning projects	50%	5%
Human resources management	16%	15%	15%	Mobilizing and allocating human resources	50%	8%
				Managing skills	50%	8%

Table 3.3. *Weighting of joint dimensions/activities*

These results show that the practices with an equivalent and relatively high weight in terms of both innovation and exporting concern strategy, customer relationship management, networking and human resources management. The practices with a high weight in terms of innovation and a low weight in terms of exporting are mainly related to knowledge management. Conversely, the practices that are essential for exporting and secondary for innovation concern company culture and project management. Finally, the practices with a medium or low weighting for both innovation and exporting correspond to intellectual property management and market/technology intelligence. In view of the results obtained, it seems that the most important dimensions with an impact on innovation concern access to knowledge and its exploitation, while those with an impact on exports favor changes in internal operations and culture.

3.2.2.2. *The calculation of a global index and the sorting process*

Finally, a sorting method was used to provide an overall index that aggregates the assessments of each company's practices and classifies them into a category that reflects its innovation (passive/reactive/preactive/proactive) and exporting (homebody/traveler/explorer/adventurer) behaviors (see Figure 3.6).

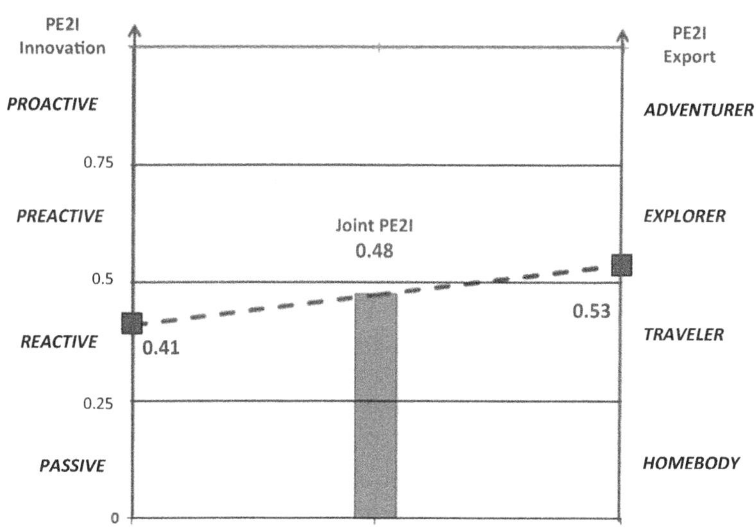

Figure 3.6. *PE2I aggregation (example)*

Suppose that the results presented in Figure 3.6 belong to a fictitious company. The evaluated company has an average joint innovation–export capability (joint PE2I = 0.48); however, it appears that this company has a predisposition to export. The triple weighting of the mathematical model highlights that its export-oriented PE2I (0.53) is higher than its innovation-oriented PE2I (0.41). This means that this company masters practices that are very important for exporting, rather than those that are important for innovation. In this case, this difference is particularly marked because the company belongs to the "explorer" category for exporting (third category) and to the "reactive" category for innovation (second category).

3.2.3. *Step 3: identify customized improvement paths*

Based on the company's profile and its three PE2I indexes, personalized recommendations can finally be proposed to improve its innovation and export capabilities. The identification of the company's weaknesses and potential predispositions, as well as the consideration of its strategy, allows the definition of a progress plan that is as realistic as possible. Three standard improvement strategies have been identified: a scenario favoring innovation, a scenario favoring export and, finally, a joint scenario (see Figure 3.7).

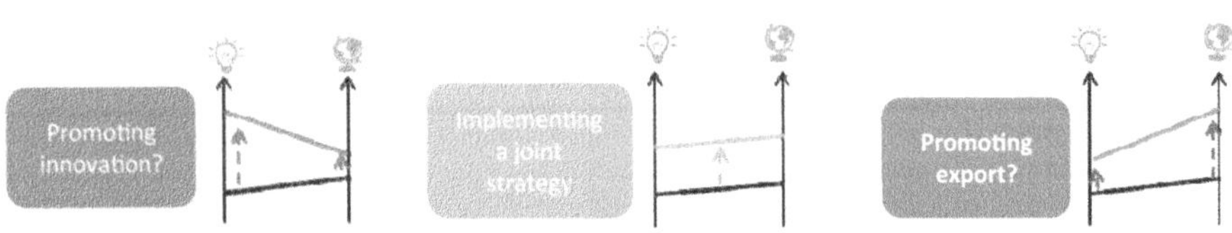

Figure 3.7. *Comparison of improvement scenarios*

The first scenario consists of choosing an orientation towards innovation. This scenario aims to improve the degree of maturity of the practices that are of great importance for the company's innovation capacity. The objective is to identify, among the weak points of the evaluated company, the practices that are particularly important for innovation and to encourage the company to improve them as a priority. These innovation-oriented practices mainly concern knowledge management, customer relations, networking and human resources management (see Table 3.3, the innovation-oriented weighting). With this scenario, the company simultaneously improves its innovation and export capabilities, but it favors innovation. This improvement scenario can be applied, for example, to a company that shows a strong export predisposition and wishes to rebalance its profile by improving innovation. This scenario can also be applied to a highly innovative company that wishes to reinforce this strategic positioning while improving, to a lesser extent, its export capacity.

The second scenario is to choose an export orientation. This scenario aims to improve practices that are particularly important for exporting: strategy, human resource management, project management and networking (see Table 3.3, the export weightings). By choosing this scenario, the company simultaneously improves its innovation and export capabilities but gives priority to its international activity. This scenario can be applied, among others, to a young exporting company that seeks to introduce or strengthen its international development.

The third scenario is to choose a joint innovation–export improvement strategy. This scenario proposes to focus on practices that are important for both export and innovation. These synergistic practices relate mainly to strategy, human resource management, networking and customer relations. This scenario is suitable, for example, for companies with very few resources and a rather low valuation. By choosing this scenario, they can make progress in both areas by optimizing the mobilization of their resources.

The definition of personalized improvement paths through the development of a progress plan associated with each scenario represents the final phase of the operational development of the PE2I assessment tool. This operational development leads to a diagnostic tool that allows evaluating SMEs' innovation and export capabilities, acting also as a decision-making tool proposing concrete actions. An Excel model of this tool has been modeled to allow its operational implementation.

To carry out this diagnosis, an external evaluator assigns a score between 1 and 5 to each joint innovation–export activity during an interview with the manager of the SME being evaluated, based on the proposed maturity grids. The evaluator then enters these ratings into the tool, which builds the company's profile in an immediate and automated way. Indeed, the tool has been designed to reduce the evaluator's manipulations to a minimum. Following this first assessment, a progress plan is proposed to the company manager, depending on the chosen improvement scenario (innovation, export or joint) and the resources available (on how many joint activities can/want to act?). The progress plan is also calculated automatically so as to offer the company director an immediate result that can be discussed during the interview. To go further, the maturity grids associated with each joint activity can be used as a basis for discussion to propose concrete recommendations. The progress plan proposes a progression in joint activity X? Let us look at the level of the maturity grid associated with this activity and what the company must do to reach the next level.

4

Implementation of the PE2I: Test with French SMEs

The PE2I, because of its design methodology, is based on both theoretical and field data; however, it is nevertheless essential to compare it to the reality of the business world, and more particularly to the SMEs, to attest to its relevance and acceptability. The aim of this application is to test its functioning in a real situation, as well as to compare the results it proposes with the vision of company managers. We have therefore carried out this application with six SMEs with different profiles.

4.1. Experimental panel and methodology

The objective of this section is to present the methodology used to implement the PE2I within SMEs. We have chosen to proceed by case study. Case study is a qualitative research method. According to Yin (2013), it is a research strategy using empirical investigation situated in a real context. It seeks to understand a contemporary phenomenon and mobilizes multiple sources of information. It is traditionally used in an exploratory manner, but according to Hlady-Rispal (2016), its contributions can be much more numerous. For this study, the case study is used in a deductive qualitative logic. It is about confronting a "theoretical" model (the PE2I tool) with the reality of the field for which it was designed (SMEs). The objective of this confrontation is twofold. First, it is a test of the PE2I in a real situation. This test concerns first the operational aspects of the tool: Does it work properly? Is it easy to use? However, this test also represents a way to test the relevance of the results proposed by the PE2I, as well as to obtain feedback from company managers on this tool: Does it meet their needs and expectations?

4.1.1. *Presentation of the panel*

Six companies have been identified to test the PE2I in a real situation. All are located in the Grand Est region (in France). Three of them are manufacturing companies; the other three are process companies. We define process SMEs as companies having a physical–chemical and/or biological transformation activity of raw materials based on a process defined by different unit operations (e.g. chemical industry, food industry and bio-industry). Manufacturing SMEs are defined as companies that produce goods by assembly (manufacture of machinery, equipment, electronics, automobiles, etc.). Unlike process enterprises, manufacturing enterprises produce goods that can be dismantled. The manufacturing process is reversible (Potier *et al.* 2015). Within these two sectors, the selected companies each represent different technological intensities (Hatzichronoglou 1997) and sizes. Thus, the PE2I was tested with two different fields of application (manufacturing and process SMEs), proposing case studies varied as well in terms of headcount, technological intensity or even export involvement.

Companies 1, 3 and 4 are in the manufacturing sector. Company 1 is a large SME in the medium-/high-tech sector. During 2014 and 2015, approximately 6% of its revenue was from exports. This company represents an interesting case study because, due to its large workforce, it should demonstrate a higher degree of structuring than smaller companies. It, therefore, provides an opportunity to test the PE2I in the case of a large SME, potentially showing a strong structuring. Companies 3 and 4 are relatively similar in size (16 and 9 employees, respectively); however, they are different in terms of technological intensity. The comparison of these two case studies can therefore highlight differences related to this characteristic. In addition, the percentage of their turnover from exports is also very different. Indeed, company 3 represents an interesting case study, as it is a company initiating its export activity. It, therefore, allows us to test the interest of PE2I for SMEs wishing to launch themselves on foreign markets.

	Sector	Workforce (2015)	Technology intensity[1]	Percentage of sales from exports (average 2014–2015)
Company 1	Manufacturer	> 200	Medium/high tech	6
Company 2	Processes	10	Low technology	4
Company 3	Manufacturer	16	Medium/high tech	1
Company 4	Manufacturer	9	High technology	53
Company 5	Processes	< 10	High technology	1
Company 6	Processes	100	Low technology	5

Table 4.1. *Presentation of the case studies*

Companies 2, 5 and 6 are process SMEs. Company 2 has a relatively small workforce (10 employees) and low technological intensity. It has an export turnover of 4%. Company 6 has a relatively similar profile in terms of technological intensity but has a much larger workforce. Its export turnover is also similar (5%). It, therefore, seems interesting to compare these two companies. Finally, company 5, however, has a very high technological intensity. On the contrary, it is a very small company. Its launch is very recent, and its international development is currently very weak.

According to Glaser and Strauss (1968), in order to be included in a sample, a case must have enough common features with other cases. The case is excluded if it has a fundamental difference.

Thus, in the case of our sample, these are common features: the companies are SMEs located in the Grand Est region, they are active in exporting and they have a product development activity. The differences are represented by the context of each of these companies (sector, size, technological intensity, etc.).

4.1.2. *The conduct of the interviews*

Each case study was conducted in the form of a semi-structured interview lasting approximately two hours. They were all conducted face to face with the manager of the company concerned. The use of an Excel model of the PE2I tool made it possible to propose interactive interviews, where the results of each phase were obtained immediately and automatically.

1 Inspired by the classification of industries according to their technological intensity (Hatzichronoglou 1997).

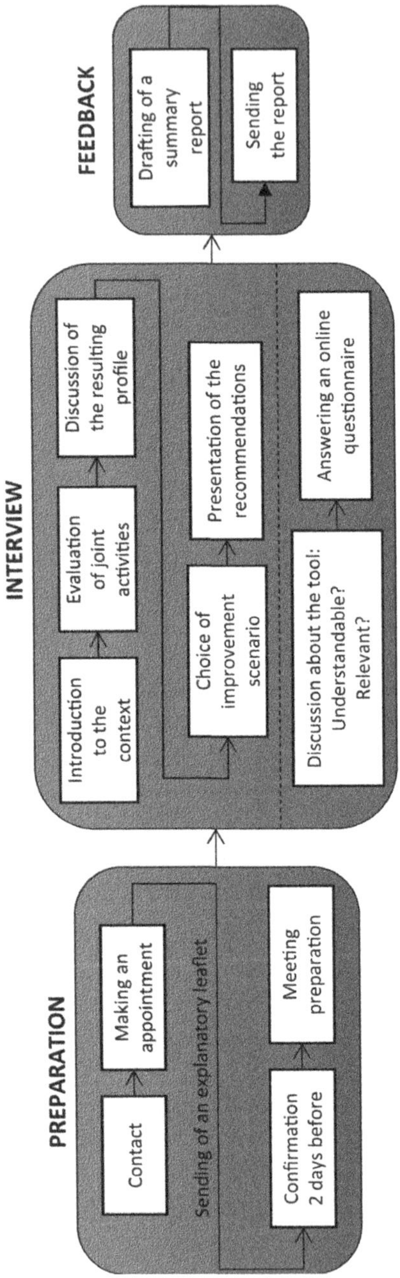

Figure 4.1. *Interview process*

The first part of the interview was devoted to evaluating the company according to the practices of the joint innovation–export reference framework. After a brief presentation of the context of our study, a discussion with the company manager allowed us to assess the company's level of maturity. A score between 1 and 5, corresponding to the level of the associated maturity grid, was attributed to each activity in order to obtain the company's profile.

An initial discussion phase was then introduced to explain the results obtained. Once the company profile was obtained, one (or more) improvement scenario(s) could be chosen by the company manager. Recommendations were then formulated and discussed based on the maturity grids of the PE2I system.

Finally, a summary report was written and sent by e-mail to the company. This report contained the detailed results obtained during the interview: the company's profile, as well as the means of improvement, envisaged according to one or more chosen scenarios.

4.2. Presentation of results and observations

The objective of this section is to present the results and observations obtained during this simulation.

The results of each company are detailed and discussed in order to assess the relevance of PE2I when confronted with the context of SMEs in the manufacturing and process sectors.

4.2.1. *Case 1: company 1*

Company 1 has more than 200 employees in the medium-/high-technology sector. It achieves 6% of its turnover from exports and has a significant R&D activity.

4.2.1.1. *The company's profile*

– A balanced and successful profile: its evaluation according to the nine joint innovation–export practices is relatively uniform (see Figure 4.2). The top image shows that company 1 has a high joint PE2I (0.87), and it seems to have a slight predisposition for innovation (its innovation-oriented PE2I is higher than its export-oriented PE2I). It is ranked in the fourth and last category both in terms of innovation (proactive) and in terms of export (adventurous). This result seems coherent, as company 1 shows a strong R&D activity associated with a long-term vision.

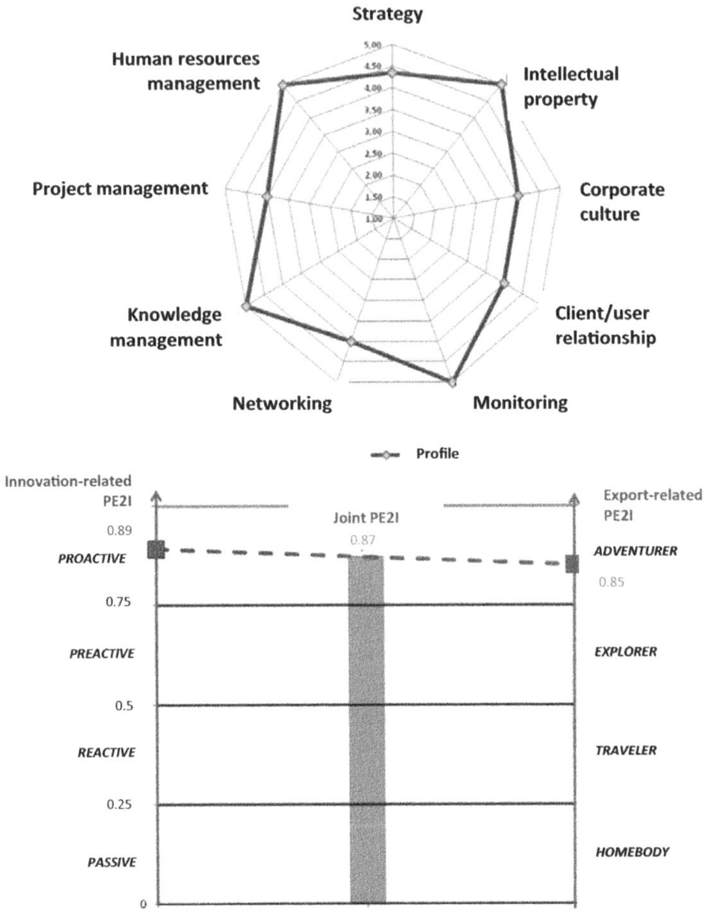

Figure 4.2. *Company profile 1. For a color version of the figure, see www.iste.co.uk/enjolras/innovation.zip*

– Its strengths: intelligence, intellectual property (IP), knowledge management and human resources management. These practices are proof of a proactive strategy and an anticipatory attitude, characteristic of proactive companies. As far as export is concerned, it has plans to develop in distant markets, both geographically and culturally. In view of this evaluation, it seems to be equipped to manage the difficulties associated with them, but improvements can be envisaged.

4.2.1.2. *The chosen improvement scenario(s): the export-oriented scenario and the joint scenario*

4.2.1.2.1. The scenario favoring export

First, the company chose to visualize the progress plan proposed by the scenario favoring export. Indeed, in view of its short-/medium-term projects, this orientation seems the most appropriate. The first critical activity identified concerns the customer/user relationship. The recommendation associated with this critical activity is to reinforce the involvement of the client/user in the project process. The second and third critical activities concern project management. This involves strengthening the management of resource allocation and the planning of the company's projects. Company 1 is planning to expand into potentially risky foreign markets. Thus, the involvement of the customer/user reduces the risks related to the acceptability of the product. Strengthening project management reduces the organizational risks associated with exporting to geographically and culturally distant markets.

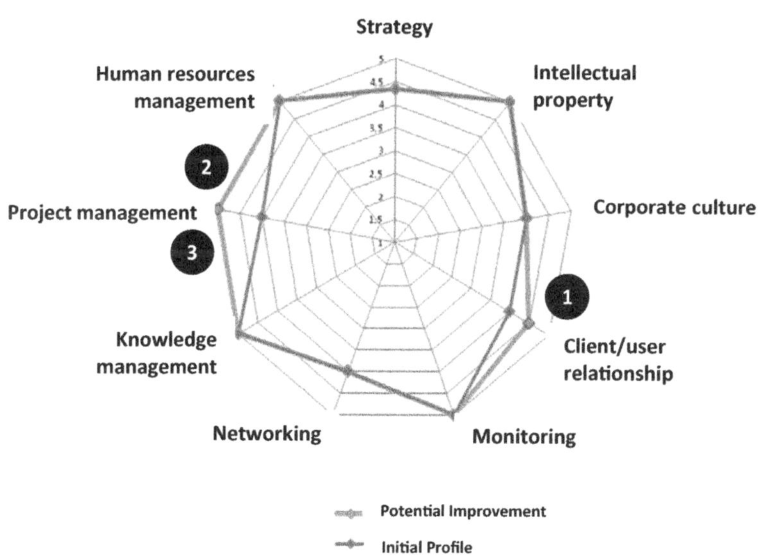

Figure 4.3A. *Potential improvement of company 1 under the export scenario. For a color version of the figure, see www.iste.co.uk/enjolras/innovation.zip*

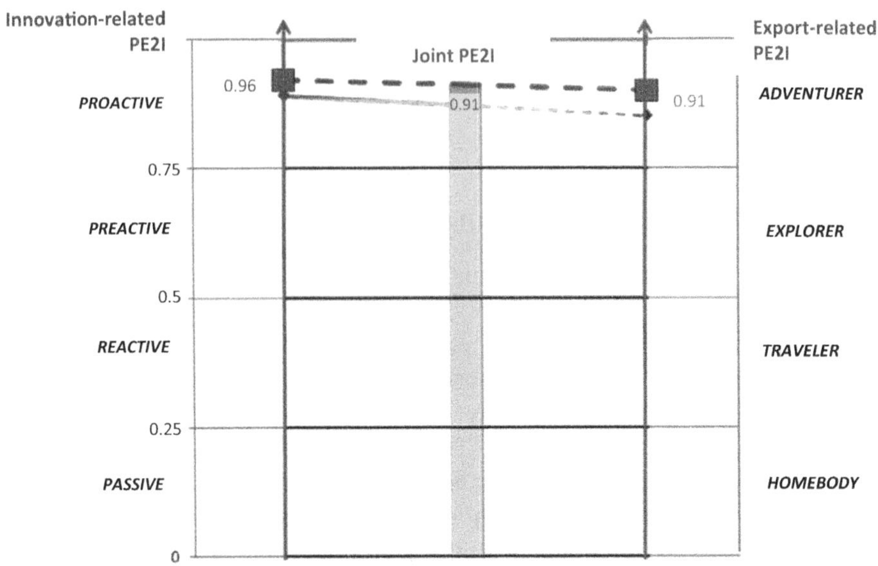

Figure 4.3B. *Potential improvement of company 1 under the export scenario (continued). For a color version of the figure, see www.iste.co.uk/enjolras/innovation.zip*

4.2.1.2.2. The joint improvement scenario

In a second step, and out of curiosity, company 1 wanted to visualize the joint innovation–export progress plan and possibly highlight synergies to be exploited. As for the export scenario, the first critical activity concerns the involvement of the customer/user in the project process. On the contrary, the second and third critical activities concern the company's networks: strong networks (suppliers, partners, distributors, etc.) and weak networks (service providers, lawyers, etc.). In view of the company's projects, the development of its network seems an appropriate recommendation since international development in difficult-to-access markets may require the establishment of partnerships and the selection of trusted distributors. On the contrary, these recommendations also improve its innovation capability and potentially allow it to differentiate itself from its competitors in the targeted markets. Thus, the joint scenario favors the acquisition of a competitive advantage, whereas the scenario favoring export aims rather at structuring the company through the formalization of its project management process.

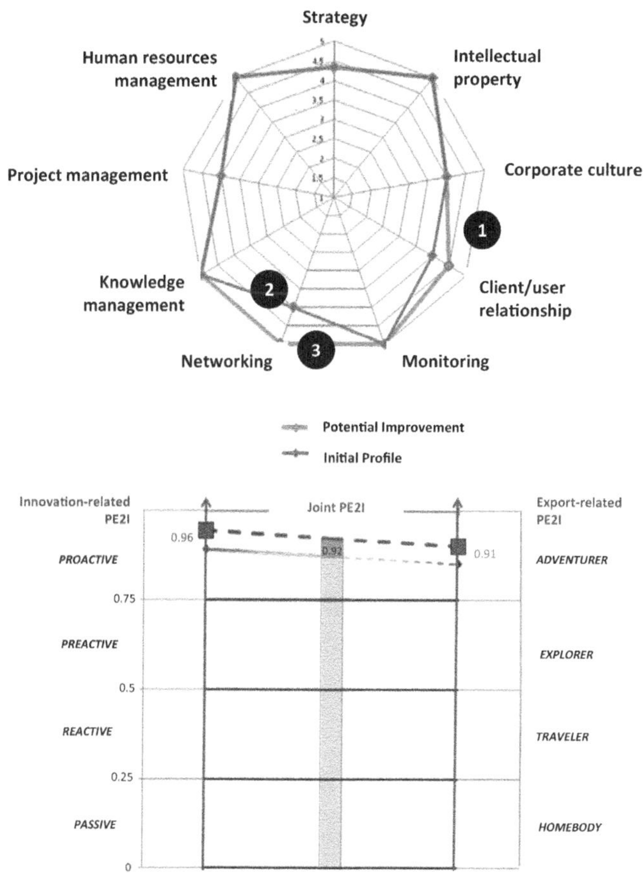

Figure 4.4. *Potential improvement of company 1 under the joint scenario. For a color version of the figure, see www.iste.co.uk/enjolras/innovation.zip*

4.2.1.3. *The observations*

Several of these recommendations were echoed by company 1. In particular, the difference between the two scenarios was noted and appreciated. The results given by the tool seem to be relevant in the case of this company, and they allow for reflection on the priority of action: Promote the acquisition of a competitive advantage or ensure formalization? The context of the company makes the formalization of the project management difficult because very few products are manufactured each year, and their number is very variable. The joint improvement scenario, therefore, seems more appropriate in the case of company 1, given its own context.

4.2.2. *Case 2: company 2*

Company 2 is a small business with 10 employees that generates 4% of its sales from exports. This company is part of the low-tech sector, which does not prevent it from regularly proposing new products that are well adapted to its national market as well as to its foreign markets.

4.2.2.1. *The company's profile*

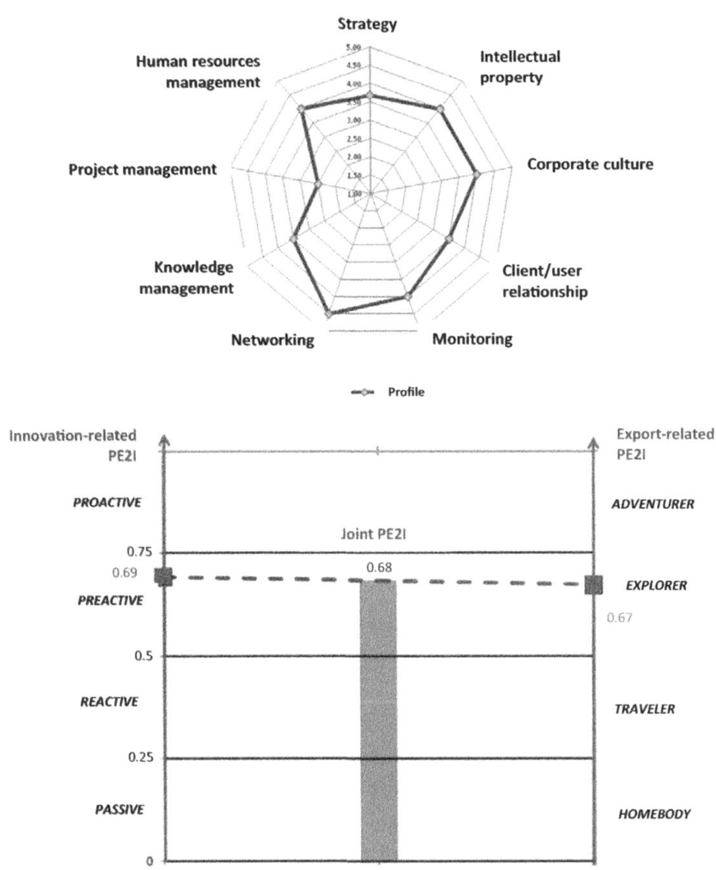

Figure 4.5. *Company profile 2. For a color version of the figure, see www.iste.co.uk/enjolras/innovation.zip*

– Despite its small size, it has a high-performance profile: it is in the third category for both export and innovation (exploratory and preactive, respectively). It is therefore capable of anticipating changes in its environment and has a medium-term vision. It is able to design new products thanks to its organization and its internal skills. It regularly exports to easily accessible countries and is able to target more distant markets, both geographically and culturally. The values of PE2I (innovation, export and joint) do not highlight any particular predisposition for one or other of these themes, and the profile of company 2 concerning the nine joint practices is globally balanced.

– A weak point: project management.

4.2.2.2. *The chosen improvement scenario(s): the scenario favoring export*

The improvement scenario chosen by the manager of company 2 concerned exports. Indeed, this is a challenge that is close to his heart and he has invested a lot of energy in it. Initially, the number of recommendations had been set at two, as the size and resources of the company were relatively limited. However, the recommendations proposed were then focused on a single practice: project management. Indeed, the main weakness of company 2 concerns the allocation of material and financial resources. A score of 2 was assigned to this activity. The PE2I, therefore, proposes recommendations that would allow the company to improve in priority on this critical activity. However, its relatively low score concerning project management comes from a lack of formalization and structuring. However, this company employs 10 people, all of whom work on the same site, and the manager is in daily contact with his employees. According to him, there is no need for formalization and structuring. This is not relevant for a small structure like his. In fact, he does not feel it is necessary to plan and budget each phase of the projects in progress, as he is in charge of managing each of them himself. The number of recommendations proposed by the tool has therefore been increased to five so that those concerning project management can be set aside and others proposed (see Figure 4.6).

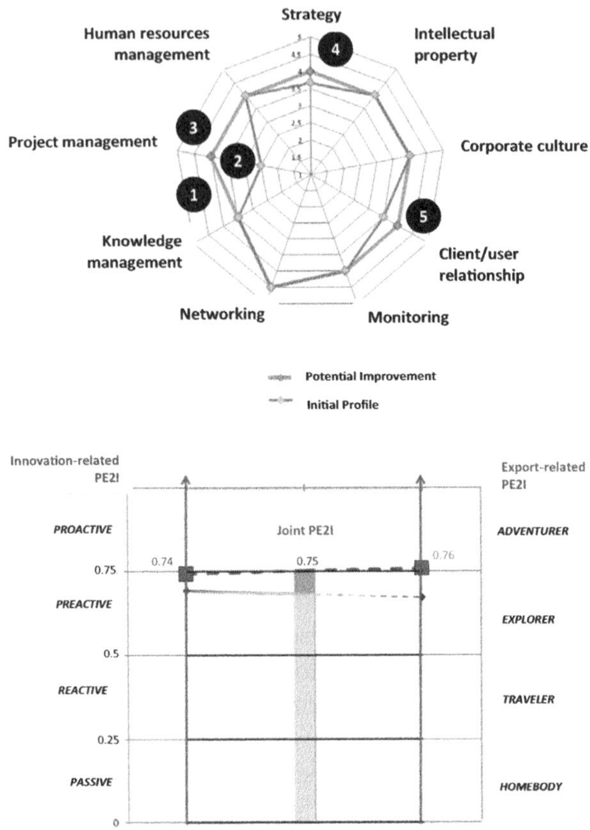

Figure 4.6. *Potential improvement of company 2 under the export scenario. For a color version of the figure, see www.iste.co.uk/enjolras/innovation.zip*

The following recommendations concerned strategy, and in particular, the positioning of the company's products through a formalized competitive analysis. The last recommendation concerned the improvement of the customer/user relationship through the involvement of customers in the project process. These last two recommendations, therefore, aim to reduce the risk linked to the acceptability of products on foreign markets, as well as to secure the company's positioning in relation to the competition.

4.2.2.3. *The observations*

This case study highlights observations that are very different from the previous case. The small size of company 2 directly impacts the perceived relevance of some of the recommendations proposed by the PE2I. This tool is based on the assumption that the level of control of companies increases with the formalization of the activities considered. However, in the case of small structures, this is questionable. Indeed, the structuring and formalization of certain activities relating to the organization of the enterprise may be considered a low priority in the particular context of small and very small enterprises since communication and management methods are much more dynamic and flexible than in the case of larger structures. For example, formalizing the sharing of information within a small structure makes little sense, on the one hand, because the means implemented to achieve this are costly in terms of time and money, but above all, because information circulates freely within small teams.

4.2.3. *Case 3: company 3*

Company 3 has 16 employees working in the medium-/high-technology sector. As a young exporter, it generates 1% of its turnover from exports and intends to gradually increase its presence on international markets.

4.2.3.1. *The company's profile*

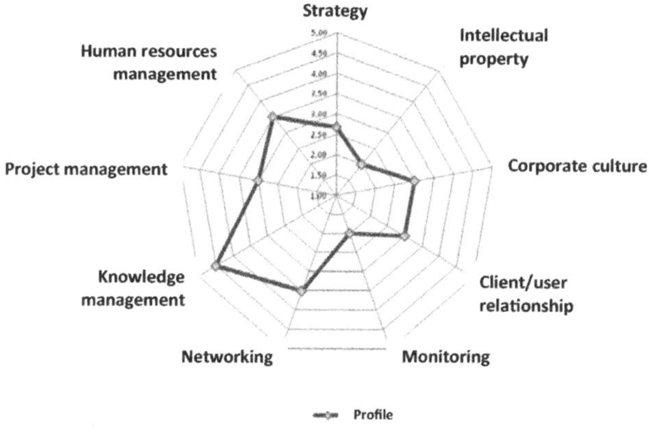

Figure 4.7A. *Company profile 3. For a color version of the figure, see www.iste.co.uk/enjolras/innovation.zip*

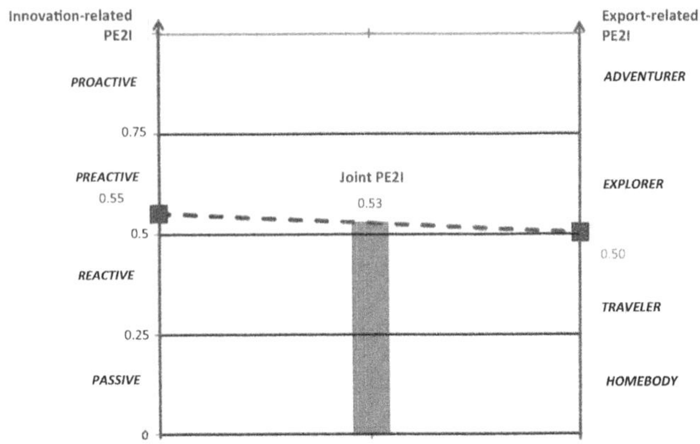

Figure 4.7B. *Company profile 3 (continued). For a color version of the figure, see www.iste.co.uk/enjolras/innovation.zip*

– Its strengths: knowledge management, networking and human resources management. These three dimensions together represent crucial dimensions for both the innovation and export capabilities. These strengths, therefore, justify the good profile of company 3 and compensate for the fact that it has a rather heterogeneous profile (see Figure 4.7).

– A good profile despite its very recent export activities: to interpret this result, it is important to specify that the PE2I does not evaluate the performance of companies; it evaluates whether the conditions necessary for their success are present within the company in the form of joint innovation–export routines/activities. Thus, although it currently exports very little, it seems to have the potential to export regularly and intensively to countries that are culturally and geographically close, and it could also consider targeting markets that are more difficult to access.

4.2.3.2. *The chosen improvement scenario(s): the scenario favoring export*

In view of the company's short- and medium-term projects, the manager's choice was quickly turned to the progress plan promoting export. The first recommendation concerns intellectual property. Indeed, it is a point to work on. However, the sector of activity of company 3 requires a particular management of the intellectual property. It is not concerned with patenting, only with software and commercial protection, which can potentially limit the importance given to this dimension. This recommendation was therefore not retained by the company, as it was not relevant in its context. The second recommendation concerns the strategy dimension and, more specifically, the prioritization of projects. Within this company, projects are managed in parallel or one after the other without any particular priority. It, therefore, seems necessary to set up a project portfolio management system, giving priority to certain projects that meet certain criteria defined by the company in accordance with its overall strategy. The third recommendation concerns customer/user relationship management and, in particular, the exploitation of customer feedback. The fourth recommendation concerns monitoring. It seems necessary to structure and formalize the information gathering process. Finally, the fifth recommendation concerns the management of human resources, and more specifically, the assignment of tasks and responsibilities.

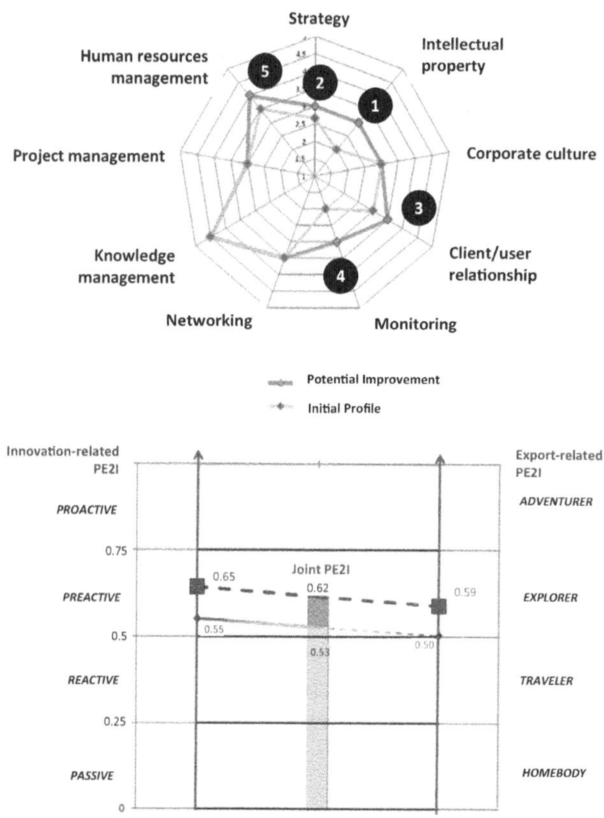

Figure 4.8. *Potential improvement of company 3 under the export scenario. For a color version of the figure, see www.iste.co.uk/enjolras/innovation.zip*

4.2.3.3. *The observations*

The recommendations proposed to the company are globally aimed at homogenizing its profile. The number one priority is intellectual property. It appears as a weak point in Figure 4.8; however, the context of company 3 calls into question this prioritization in view of the particular protection approach associated with its sector of activity. This particular case, therefore, highlights a limitation of the tool. As suggested by the contingency theory (Mintzberg 1979), there are very diverse specificities linked to the sector of activity, the environment, and many other contextual factors that must be taken into account when evaluating companies. It, therefore, seems necessary to adapt the recommendations proposed by the tool to the particular context of the company.

In view of the company's profile, its second weak point concerns monitoring. However, it is interesting to note that the second proposed action aims at improving the prioritization of the company's projects (strategy). This proves that the PE2I does not necessarily act in priority on the weak points of the evaluated companies. Depending on the chosen improvement scenario, priority will be given to the most critical activity in the context of this same scenario. Thus, in order to promote exports, it is more urgent for the company to focus on prioritizing its projects than on information gathering, even though this represents one of its weak points. A similar observation can be made regarding the fifth recommendation. The PE2I recommends that it act on the management of its internal skills, even though this is one of the company's strong points. Thus, even though the management of competencies seems relatively mastered, it must still be improved if it wishes to promote its export development.

This case study highlights several observations. First, it allows us to compare two companies of modest size (about 10 employees) from different sectors of activity: company 2 (low technology) and company 3 (medium/high technology). The difficulty related to the lack of formalization of small companies is less marked in the case of company 3, although it is still present. Indeed, some of the recommendations proposed to company 3 concern the formalization of its information search or project prioritization processes, and it would seem that they have difficulty finding an echo with its manager. This case study, therefore, confirms the lack of relevance of some of the recommendations proposed by the tool for small companies, regardless of the level of technological intensity. However, this case study highlights the need to take into account the specificities of the company's context: sector of activity, environment and so on. Certain recommendations must therefore be adapted to the specificities of the company. Some recommendations must therefore be qualified or adapted to be coherent. Finally, this case study is a good illustration of the interest of proposing different improvement scenarios. It is interesting to note that the recommendations are not exclusively aimed at homogenizing the company's profile. The action priorities are given according to the improvement scenario chosen by the company.

4.2.4. *Case 4: company 4*

Company 4 is in the high-tech sector. It has nine employees and generates half of its turnover from exports. It is located in a niche market, which makes its international development essential.

4.2.4.1. *The company's profile*

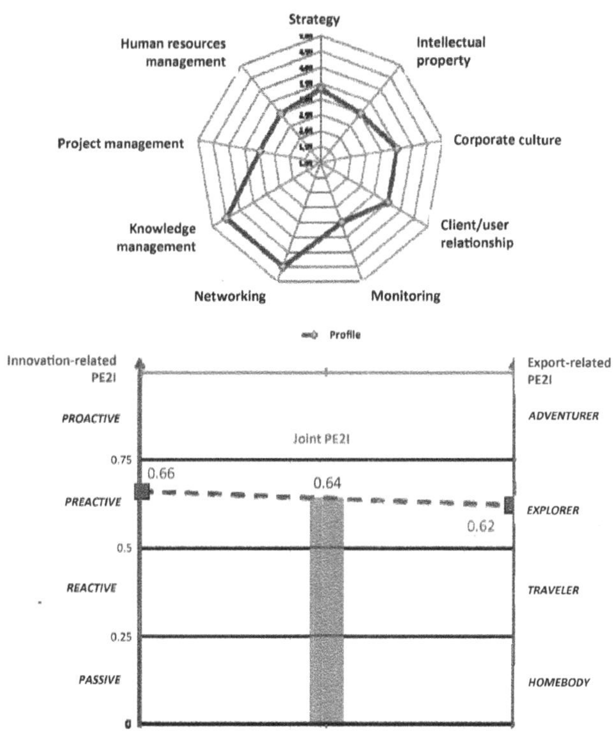

Figure 4.9. *Company profile 4. For a color version of the figure, see www.iste.co.uk/enjolras/innovation.zip*

– A homogeneous and performing profile, slightly oriented towards innovation.

– Two main strengths: knowledge management and networking. These strengths are real drivers for the company and represent pillars on which it can rely to improve its performance in terms of innovation and export.

4.2.4.2. *The chosen improvement scenario(s): the scenario favoring innovation*

Company 4 considers itself above all an innovative company. It has a strong international presence; however, this is almost an obligation due to the niche market in which it operates. Exporting is therefore not an objective in itself but rather a means to an end. Hence, the manager's choice turned to the scenario favoring innovation. The priority axis of work concerns the information gathering. Company 4's monitoring approach is intuitive, without any particular structure. It would be possible to define priority areas of research concerning its core business and its current markets in order to propose a global dynamic of information research. The second priority area of work concerns human resources management.

Intellectual property is also considered a point to work on. However, company 4 bases the protection of its products on a *first-mover* strategy. It, therefore, innovates regularly in order to outdo the competition. It has therefore chosen not to use (or to make little use of) the traditional tools of protection (patent, software protection, commercial protection, etc.). This recommendation is therefore not relevant in its particular case, since it does not resonate with its manager. Once again, it seems important to adapt the recommendations proposed by the PE2I to the specific context of the company diagnosed. Finally, customer relationship management could also be improved. Company 4 has a precise and formalized approach to customer feedback; however, customers are not very involved in the design and testing process of its products. In general, the improvement scenario that favors innovation particularly caught the attention of the manager. The proposed improvement paths appeared to be relevant and in line with the company's vision, and this is particularly true for the recommendation concerning information retrieval. This is a point that the company wishes to work on as a priority.

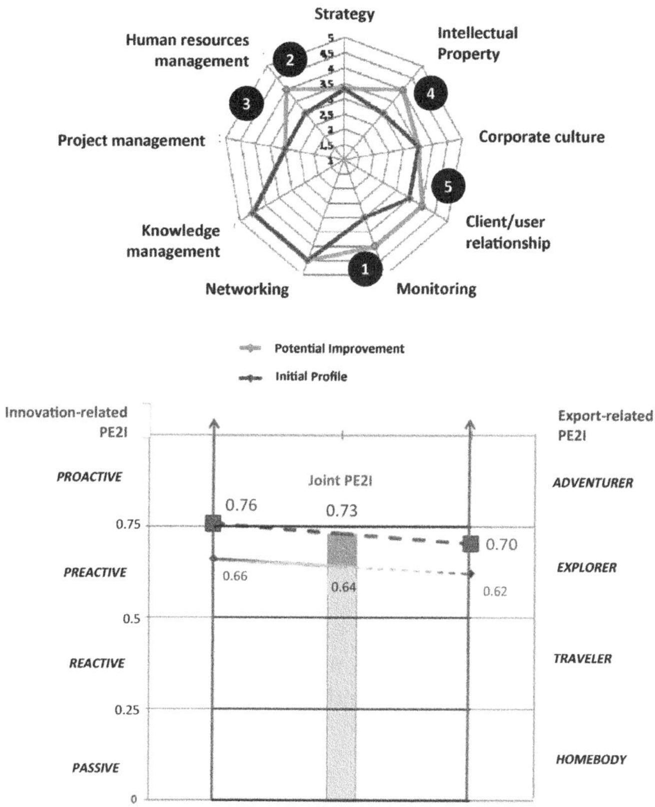

Figure 4.10. *Potential improvement in company 4 under the innovation scenario. For a color version of the figure, see www.iste.co.uk/enjolras/innovation.zip*

4.2.4.3. *The observations*

This case study allows us once again to evaluate the relevance of the PE2I results for a small company. The main difference with the two previous cases (see sections 4.2.2 and 4.2.3) concerns the sector of activity of the company. Indeed, it is a high-tech SME, which is inherently international due to its niche market. The comparison with companies 2 and 3 is interesting because, despite their differences, the formalization problem is present in each of them.

Company 4 is also confronted with this limitation through the need to formalize its monitoring process. It also considers this difficulty to be a necessary area for improvement in the more or less short term. It, therefore, seems that the recommendations concerning formalization and structuring, in general, are considered more relevant in the case of company 4 than for companies 3 or 2. The recommendations were echoed where the managers of companies 2 and 3 had little interest in them. This can be explained either by the difference in the sector of activity (high tech) or by the intensity of exports. In fact, unlike companies 2 and 3, company 4 achieves 50% of its turnover from exports. It, therefore, exports on a regular and intensive basis, which potentially requires greater formalization and structuring.

In general, this diagnosis allowed company 4 to take the time to reflect on intuitively known elements (the identified strengths and weaknesses being in agreement with the vision of the manager). The PE2I appeared to be a good formalization tool. The joint innovation–export vision was particularly appreciated, as it allows a global approach to the problems the company is facing.

4.2.5. *Case 5: company 5*

Company 5 was created in 2012 in the high-tech process sector. It has a staff of less than 10 people and is currently beginning its export development.

4.2.5.1. *The company's profile*

– Two main strengths: intellectual property and corporate culture. As a young high-tech company, these strengths are really at the heart of the company's operations. Patent filing, IP rights monitoring, autonomy and initiative-taking are all fundamentals that allow company 4 to show a good profile both in terms of innovation and export, despite its recent creation.

– A slightly export-oriented profile: the company currently generates less than 1% of its sales from exports. However, its export PE2I is very good. Once again, it is necessary to specify that the PE2I measures the potential capacity of a company to innovate and export. Therefore, this result does not allow us to judge the performance of company 5 in exporting but to highlight an important predisposition. The company is "exploratory" and is therefore potentially capable of exporting regularly and intensively to countries that are culturally and geographically close to it, and it is also capable of targeting a few countries that are more difficult to access.

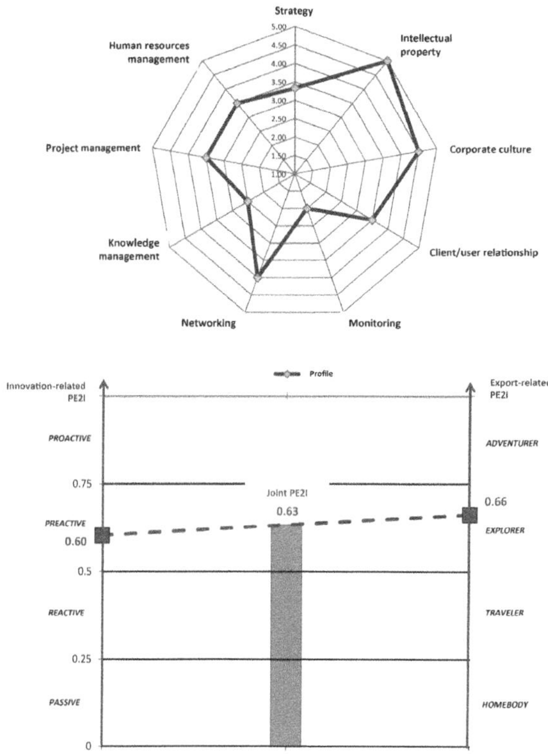

Figure 4.11. *Company profile 5. For a color version of the figure, see www.iste.co.uk/enjolras/innovation.zip*

4.2.5.2. The chosen improvement scenario(s): the export-oriented scenario

As the company is currently beginning its export development, the choice of a progress plan to consider export appeared naturally. Company 5's priority area of work concerns customer relationship management. The implementation of a customer information collection process (satisfaction, customer feedback, opinions, etc.) seems particularly interesting in the context of export development, in order to identify ways of improving products, cultural differences to be taken into account or reticence specific to a particular market. The second priority area of work concerns information gathering. The implementation of a structured monitoring approach, coupled with the company's strong control of intellectual property, could be interesting from both a market and technological point of view. The third axis of work is related to the management of human resources and, more precisely, to the management of competencies: proactive recruitment, identification and valorization of training. Finally, the last axis of work concerns project management, and more particularly, planning. These last two areas of work highlight a lack of formalization and structuring of processes; however, this is largely due to the fact that the company is very new. The implementation of a proactive vision of training and recruitment is partly hindered by the difficulty of considering the company's long-term situation. In the same way, it seems difficult to implement a planned and equipped project management process at this stage of development, among other things, because of a lack of financial resources and time.

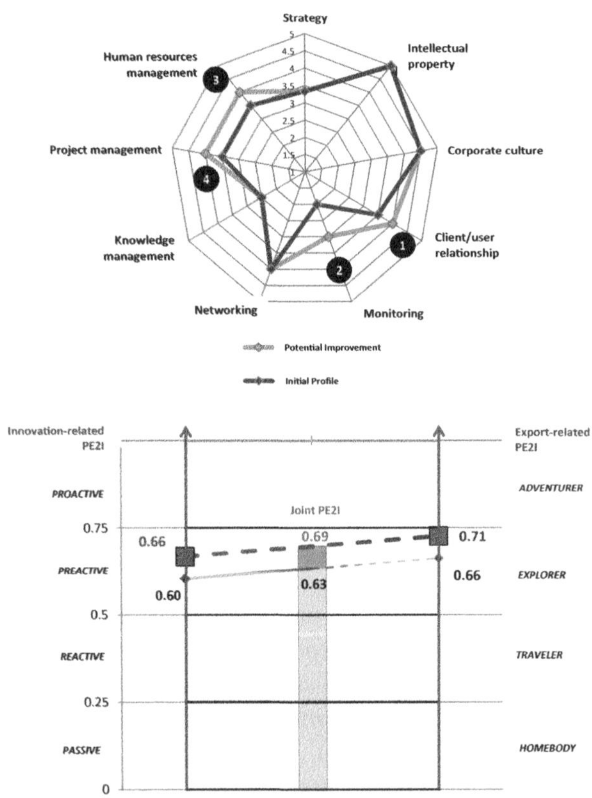

Figure 4.12. *Potential improvement of company 5 under the export scenario. For a color version of the figure, see www.iste.co.uk/enjolras/innovation.zip*

4.2.5.3. *The observations*

This case study allows us to evaluate the relevance of the PE2I results for an SME with a profile that, at first glance, is similar to that of company 4: a high-tech SME with a relatively small workforce. However, there are important differences. First, company 5 is a process SME, unlike company 4, which is a manufacturing company. Second, company 5 was recently created and is currently beginning its international development. The comparison with company 4 is interesting because, despite their differences, the problem of formalization is present in both of them. However, in the case of company 5, the difficulty in formalizing and structuring processes affects the vast majority of the practices evaluated. However, given its recent creation, this can be explained. In general, this diagnosis enabled it to obtain a vision of its profile at a given moment. This aspect appeared interesting to the manager. However, more concrete recommendations would have been appreciated.

Three important points were highlighted by this case study. First, despite a low level of export development (less than 1% of its turnover), company 5 has a high export-oriented PE2I. This result is a concrete illustration of the bias of this study, which consists of evaluating the potential capacity of a company to innovate and export, and not its performance. In the case of company 5, this result bodes well for its export development, as it seems ready to export regularly and to countries that are more or less easy to access. On the contrary, this evaluation clearly highlighted a weak point concerning knowledge management and intelligence (see Figure 4.12). However, in the recommendation phase, monitoring comes in second place, and knowledge management is not considered a priority area of work. Thus, depending on the improvement scenario chosen, the PE2I does not necessarily push companies to act on their weak points. It contextualizes the recommendations according to the chosen strategy.

Finally, a limitation to the PE2I recommendations appears to be apparent. This limit is directly linked to the resources available. Indeed, in the case of company 5, the lack of formalization and structuring is, in most cases, linked to a lack of time or financial means. The PE2I focuses its evaluation on internal practices; however, they are obviously dependent on the means that the company is able to raise. The importance of resources, in a context linked to SMEs, is therefore highlighted by this case study, as it directly impacts their ability to implement the proposed recommendations.

4.2.6. *Case 6: company 6*

Company 6 is a process company with low technological intensity. It employs about 100 people and generates 5% of its turnover from exports. Its ambition is to increase this figure in the near future.

4.2.6.1. *The company's profile*

– A very homogeneous profile at first sight, with a clear driving force: networking.

– However, when we look at the activities defining each of the dimensions evaluated, the profile is much less homogeneous. Within the same practice, some activities are very well mastered; others are much less so. This is notably the case for the practices of customer relationship management, strategy and knowledge management. The representation chosen to visualize the company's profile is based on an average calculation, so these heterogeneities are smoothed out.

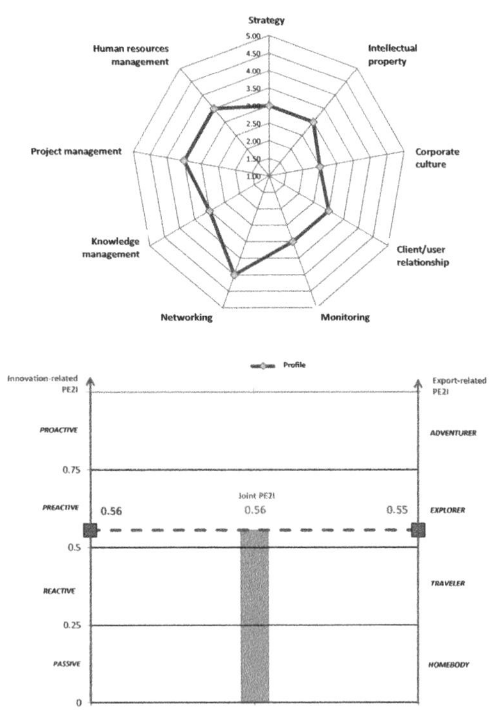

Figure 4.13. *Company profile 6. For a color version of the figure, see www.iste.co.uk/enjolras/innovation.zip*

4.2.6.2. *The chosen improvement scenario(s): the export-oriented scenario*

With the objective of developing its international activity, the first area of work identified by the tool concerns the theme of the company's culture. This theme evaluates the proactivity and initiative of employees as well as the presence or absence of conditions that facilitate exchanges between departments and/or individuals. Thus, despite the strong involvement of employees in their work and their attachment to the company, a strong resistance to change seems to appear. Hence, this issue seems particularly critical. However, this recommendation was deemed inappropriate by the manager because in view of the very conservative context linked to the company's sector of activity, the proactivity of employees is not necessarily sought after. Hence, we have omitted this aspect for the rest of the diagnosis.

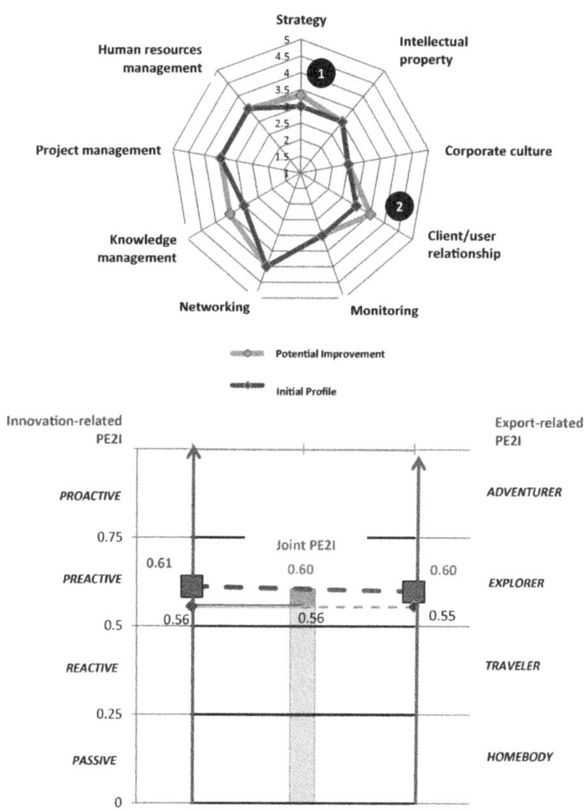

Figure 4.14. *Potential improvement of company 6 under the export scenario. For a color version of the figure, see www.iste.co.uk/onjolras/innovation.zip*

The priority area of work, therefore, concerns strategy. More specifically, company 6 has a good command of its commercial positioning on its various markets; however, its overall strategy could be more formalized. The main orientations are defined; however, the notion of opportunity plays an important role in the company's operations, which can be a handicap in the long term. The use of strategic analysis tools (market research, risk analysis, etc.) could facilitate this approach. The second area of work concerns the involvement of customers (and/or distributors, importers, etc.), both in the creation of new products and in the identification of potentially promising markets. The company's strong capacity for networking could be a major asset on which to rely for this approach. Finally, the sharing and exploitation of knowledge could be improved through the implementation of a dissemination process. Attempts have already been made to test collaborative digital tools. It would seem that this is an avenue to pursue.

4.2.6.3. *The observations*

This case study allows us to evaluate once again the relevance of the PE2I results, this time in the case of an SME with a large workforce. This case can be easily compared to that of company 2, also a process and low-tech SME, which achieves 4% of its turnover from exports. The main difference between these two companies is the number of employees (about ten for company 2 and about a hundred for company 6). However, the profiles of these two companies are rather different. Company 2 shows a better innovation and export capability, despite its small size. However, the recommendations proposed by the tool are relatively similar. They relate in particular to formalization difficulties. It would therefore seem that these difficulties are not exclusively experienced by small companies.

In general, the improvement paths proposed to company 6 appeared to be relevant and in line with the company's vision (apart from the one related to the company's culture). The manager was surprised, however, not to see project management as a potential area for improvement. This can be explained by the fact that this practice is characteristic of the hidden heterogeneity of the company's profile, because of the two activities that make up this practice, one was judged to be very well mastered (allocation of financial and material resources) while the other was much less so (project planning). This practice, therefore, obtains an average score, which explains why it does not appear, at first glance, as a weak point (see Figure 4.14). This may be a limitation of the tool, as the representation of themes in radar tends to smooth out heterogeneities. On the contrary, the weighting given to the "project management" theme is weak from an export point of view. It is not a critical dimension. Thus, the activity of "project planning", which is not very well mastered, does not appear as a recommendation in the improvement scenario for export. However, it could appear in the case of the improvement scenario promoting innovation.

4.3. Assessment

These six case studies made it possible to apply the PE2I and to confront it with the vision of manufacturing and process SMEs in the Grand Est region. The different companies evaluated were of different sizes and sectors of activity, had a more or less strong export activity and showed a variable technological intensity. In general, this tool was well received by company managers. The theme clearly aroused their interest, and the tool itself also aroused their curiosity. During the interview, the managers of the six companies evaluated all wanted to test several improvement scenarios in order to visualize the tool's potential. They spontaneously gave their opinion on the tool, and some were challenged by the results of their evaluation. Generally speaking, the tool raises questions among managers by provoking them to take a step back from the way their company operates.

Given the limited number of applications, this test cannot be used as a validation of the tool's relevance. However, it can highlight trends and limits to be explored for future developments.

The main points of vigilance raised during this experimentation refer, on the one hand, to the question of the formalization of processes in SMEs: Is this always a necessity or could it prove counterproductive in the case of small structures? Indeed, it seems questionable to propose to a company of five employees to set up a formalized and structured system of information sharing, given that information circulates freely within the company. In addition, the question of the availability of the necessary resources for the formalization of these processes within small companies (notably in terms of time and financial means) was also addressed. On the other hand, the question of context, through the sector of activity, the size and the operating mode of the companies, appears to be a strong differentiating factor to be taken into account in the proposed recommendations. This situation has arisen several times, particularly with regard to the practice of managing intellectual property. Indeed, this practice is approached in a particularly heterogeneous way within SMEs, as was pointed out in Chapter 3. Thus, it seems necessary to adopt a contingent vision of the practices evaluated and to find a compromise between the standardization necessary for the design of a decision support tool and the intrinsic specificity of the context in which each company evolves.

5

Feedback on the PE2I Tool

Following the confrontation of the PE2I with a panel of SMEs, several advantages and limits were highlighted. This chapter provides feedback on these implementations and opens the way to different work perspectives.

Thus, the positive points of the tool that were put forward mainly concern its ability to provide a clear and relevant overview of the company's practices. Indeed, it appears as a strategic visualization tool with an educational scope because it allows the manager to "put on paper" elements that are generally intuitive but not verbalized. In this way, the PE2I fulfills its role as a decision-making tool.

On the contrary, the tests we conducted raised elements of the tool's evaluation process that could imply operational problems. For example, it seems that the proposed tool lacks the flexibility and adaptability to offer companies a truly personalized assessment, despite its initial ambition. It was also stressed during the tests that a contact person was essential to interpret the joint innovation–export results of the diagnosis. The operational implementation of the diagnosis is therefore made difficult by the complexity of the analysis and the results it proposes.

5.1. The advantages and limitations of the PE2I tool

5.1.1. *A customizable pedagogical representation tool*

The PE2I is a tool initially intended to act directly within companies to improve their situation by offering them operational recommendations. It is therefore rather positivist in its positioning. However, the tests carried out have highlighted the educational purpose of this tool.

The PE2I leads the manager to question his own situation, and this is one of its main advantages. Indeed, the tool allows them to compile and visually represent knowledge that they already possess in an implicit and intuitive way. Thus, the PE2I appears as a pedagogical and didactic tool allowing an objectification of the situation. It is not only a support tool aimed at improving the performance of companies, but above all, a decision-making tool for its manager, allowing them to confirm their intuitions or to take a step back from their situation. This tool puts the manager at the heart of the evaluation process, providing support in defining his or her improvement strategy over the long term.

The second advantage of PE2I is the compromise it proposes between inclusion and customization. Indeed, PE2I is "generic" in the sense that it is based on best innovation and export practices that are considered as standard, and therefore potentially applicable in any type of company. This is indeed the bias of this work. Moreover, by focusing its evaluation not on the performance of companies in terms of innovation and export but on their potential to create favorable conditions, the inclusive nature of the tool is increased 10-fold.

In fact, it is aimed at both highly innovative SMEs that are well established in their international markets and more traditional SMEs that are first-time exporters. This approach has the advantage of being stimulating for companies because even a company that is new to innovation and exporting can still obtain a good profile through this evaluation if it demonstrates an ability to create favorable conditions for its development strategies. To this end, the PE2I is an inclusive and generic tool.

However, one of its particularities lies in the different improvement scenarios it offers. This makes it an adaptive tool that can be customized on a case-by-case basis. The possibility of choosing the improvement scenario allows the company manager to be involved in the evaluation and helps to contextualize and personalize the evaluation. The main objective of this choice of scenario is to give meaning to the evaluation. Most of the managers we met during the case studies wanted to see several scenarios in order to compare them. The differences between the scenarios were generally interesting and made sense to the business leaders. In addition, the fact that the recommendations proposed by the tool differ according to the improvement scenario chosen lends credibility to the tool: it is not simply a matter of homogenizing the company's profile by acting primarily on its weak points. It is about proposing relevant recommendations in view of the chosen strategy. In this way, the PE2I can be qualified as a decision-making tool with an educational and inclusive scope while offering a personalization that reflects a desire to get as close as possible to the reality of each company evaluated.

5.1.2. *Operational difficulties*

The PE2I has a strong theoretical ambition. It proposes the evaluation of a common innovation–export space translating the complex relationship between these activities. And because of its inclusive nature, it proposes a standardized evaluation of companies while highlighting priorities for action that allow for a personalization of the recommendations to be implemented. Thus, this tool aims to propose a simultaneous evaluation of SMEs' innovation and export capabilities through a complex vision of this relationship and a consensual positioning between standardization and specificity. However, the tests carried out in real-life situations have highlighted certain operational difficulties in implementing this theoretical ambition.

First, the main operational difficulty identified lies in the way the diagnosis is administered. Indeed, the PE2I provides a simultaneous and joint vision of innovation and export activities within SMEs. However, within these same companies, the people in charge of innovation and export are generally not the same (except within the smallest structures for which the manager himself manages both activities). Thus, while innovation is generally managed by the technical or R&D departments when they exist, international activities are the responsibility of the sales department. The interlocutors are, therefore, potentially multiple and may have different points of view on the actions carried out on a daily basis. Indeed, when questioning one or the other, the discussion systematically takes an orientation depending on the interlocutor's field of expertise.

In an attempt to overcome this methodological difficulty, all of our interviews were conducted with the company manager in order to base our evaluation on his overall vision of the company. Nevertheless, it was difficult to maintain a joint vision of these two activities while talking about very concrete actions carried out within the company. Depending on the sensitivity of each person, priority was systematically given either to innovation or to export. The joint innovation–export vision, therefore, requires intellectual gymnastics and a high degree of abstraction to interpret and evaluate organizational routines that are often dedicated to one or the other of these activities. For this reason, each interview was conducted face-to-face in order to guarantee this joint vision, which relied exclusively on the specific skills of the evaluator to conduct the interview.

The joint practice assessment phase is, therefore, particularly critical from an operational point of view, and the PE2I cannot be used as a self-evaluation in its current version. It requires contact between the evaluator and the evaluated, which can be time-consuming for both the company manager and the potential support institution that would provide this diagnosis.

On the contrary, the case studies raised the problem of the adaptability of the recommendations proposed by the PE2I. Indeed, most of the case studies presented specificities linked either to the activity sector of the evaluated company, or to its environment, or to its own strategic positioning. The relevance of intellectual property management, the planning of project processes or the type of relationship maintained with clients are all issues that required case-by-case treatment during the tests carried out when it was a question of identifying possible ways of improvement for the company. Thus, the specificity of each company sometimes makes it difficult to propose operational recommendations because they are not realistic or not adapted to certain characteristics specific to the context in which the company evolves.

This is particularly evident in the diversity of the business sectors represented, each of which has its own way of implementing the innovation and export practices evaluated. However, it is also reflected in a more general way, through the internal functioning of companies.

Indeed, the tool is based on the hypothesis that the formalization and structuring of innovation and export activities within companies improve their capacity to innovate and export. In Chapter 1, we developed the notion of "denaturation" of SMEs (Torrès and Julien 2005), according to which innovation and exporting push SMEs to acquire internal processes similar to those of larger companies.

However, the issue of structuring and formalization in SMEs is a much-debated research topic. There are a few empirical studies on this subject, and it is difficult to find a consensus. Calori *et al.* (1997) studied French SMEs and found that 30% of them practiced strategic planning with a high degree of anticipation and formalization. Thus, although their practices are different from those of large companies, some SMEs plan, formalize and structure their internal organization (Goy and Paturel 2004). A study by García Pérez de Lema *et al.* (2012) conducted on a sample of more than 1,000 Spanish SMEs reveals that SMEs using formalization and strategic planning tools perform better than others. These results also show that the structuring of SMEs increases with, among other things, the size and age of the company, its technological intensity and the level of education of its manager.

Thus, the hypothesis according to which the formalization and planning of internal activities are synonymous with good control over them can be considered valid; however, it must be qualified according to the context of the company. For example, some SMEs compensate for their lack of formalization by operating intuitively, based on a long-term vision and anticipation (Sauner-Leroy 2000). Moreover, in the particular case of very small structures, formalization does not always seem necessary, given their compact spatial configuration (Torrès 2015).

Thus, the tendency to encourage companies to formalize and structure their internal processes, whatever their mode of operation and characteristics, is sometimes not welcomed by company managers who do not see the point. However, this encouragement to structure and formalize can appear to be a means of anticipating the company's future growth by providing elements for reflection on the next steps that the company may have to take. In any case, this "structuring" vision sometimes poses problems of adequacy with the context of the company, in the same way as certain sector-dependent recommendations.

Finally, when the personalized progress plans were proposed to companies, company managers regularly expressed the need for concrete recommendations. In its current state of development, the PE2I makes it possible to propose avenues for improvement in the form of general guidelines, but these do not go as far as proposing an operational action plan.

It is only a matter of identifying certain dysfunctions and suggesting action levers based on the maturity grids on which the joint practices framework is based. One of the main results of the tests carried out is the need to operationalize the recommendations made to the companies in order to propose concrete solutions, possibly by putting them in contact with targeted support organizations.

Thus, the main operational limits of the PE2I lie in its complexity of implementation (due to the joint vision it imposes) and in its relatively fixed and abstract system of recommendations (due to its consensual positioning between standardization and personalization). After having tested it in a real situation, it appears that it is difficult to evaluate practices without a trained evaluator who is able to integrate and combine the statements made by the manager with an innovation or export bias. The complexity of the innovation–export relationship and the compartmentalization of these activities within companies makes it difficult to evaluate joint practices in the field. Moreover, the proposed tool lacks the flexibility and adaptability to propose a concrete and truly personalized progress plan to the evaluated companies. The limited number of case studies carried out does not really allow us to take a position; however, it seems necessary to find a balance between the ease of implementation of the evaluation, its capacity for inclusion and the adaptability of the proposed recommendations.

5.2. Prospects for improvement

In order to take into account the limitations previously identified, several avenues for improvement were considered. The tool has been tested in two different application fields (manufacturing and process SMEs) and the results obtained seem to attest to a certain consistency. However, in order to move from the experimental stage (prototype tool) to the development stage of an operational tool that can be disseminated on a large scale, certain improvements must be considered. This section, therefore, identifies the development avenues to be explored in order to act on three main issues:

– facilitating the operational implementation of the evaluation while ensuring the joint vision carried by the tool;

– improving the adaptability of the diagnosis and its recommendation system to the context of the companies and their specificities;

– moving towards the formulation of concrete recommendations in the form of an operational action plan.

5.2.1. *Operationalizing the evaluation: reconciling the constraints of the field*

5.2.1.1. *The innovation–export link in practice: the limits of a joint evaluation*

The first results of this research work showed the importance of existing synergies between innovation and export capabilities. The point of view chosen was, therefore, the evaluation of joint practices, acting simultaneously on innovation and export activities. However, the feedback from the PE2I prototype test showed that the evaluation required a significant mental workload to keep this simultaneity in mind. For example, if we evaluate the networking capacity within a company, the innovation and export networks are not the same, and their objectives are potentially different (technical partnership or commercial partnership). As a result, it may seem complicated to assess the company's joint capability to build and mobilize a network simultaneously and jointly. Moreover, although all of our interviews were conducted in the presence of the company director in order to take advantage of his global vision of the actions carried out within his company, it could sometimes be difficult to reach the purely operational level of the actions carried out. Indeed, the vision of the company director is generally strategic, and the evaluation of certain practices required knowledge of the routines and processes implemented on a day-to-day basis. To do this, it would have been necessary to address the issue with targeted contacts within the company in charge of innovation or in charge of managing the export process. However, this would have involved another difficulty linked to the compartmentalization of the management of innovation and export activities within companies. In fact, by interviewing an innovation manager and an export manager simultaneously, we are dealing with two different people who may have specific points of view and objectives and a certain understanding of the practices being evaluated. The question of the joint innovation–export vision at the stage of the evaluation of practices, therefore, poses a major operational difficulty due to the complexity that it intrinsically brings.

One improvement envisaged would be to evaluate separately the practices related to innovation and those related to exporting. Then, the link between innovation and exporting could be made by revealing the synergies not in terms of practices implemented but in terms of recommendations proposed to the company.

For example:

– If the company wishes to progress in terms of exporting, it could ask itself which innovation drivers it could rely on to achieve its goals: How can it optimize what it already knows to limit the necessary effort?

– If, on the contrary, it wishes to improve on a specific aspect in terms of exports, it could ask: Are synergies created?

Thus, the joint and complex vision of innovation and export would not come into play during the evaluation phase but during the construction of the progress plan. In this way, the PE2I acts as a revelation of synergies by creating bridges between innovation and export practices and by suggesting the launch of joint actions. It thus concedes part of its evaluation function in favor of its function as a support and decision-making tool.

5.2.1.2. *Facilitating the dissemination of the tool: towards a self-diagnosis*

The first tests of the tool showed that its current level of development required the presence of a trained interlocutor capable of implementing the diagnosis in order to clarify and interpret the results. Indeed, the diagnoses were carried out during two-hour face-to-face interviews. However, if we pursue the orientation proposed in section 5.2.1.1, and if we choose to propose a differentiated evaluation of innovation and export practices, the time dedicated to the evaluation would only be longer. Thus, in the perspective of a massive dissemination of this tool to companies, this type of implementation does not seem optimal, as it is very time-consuming.

One of the perspectives of this work concerns the evolution of the PE2I towards an online self-assessment distributed via a Web platform. The main difficulty highlighted by this self-evaluation is the objectivity of the answers given by the respondent. This subjectivity can intervene at the level of the understanding of the questions asked, as well as at the level of the answer itself.

The PE2I is based on the principle of a maturity grid, with each practice evaluated described in text form according to five progressive levels reflecting a certain mastery of the practice in question. The objective is to position the company on the level of the maturity grid that corresponds to its situation. A format based on self-assessment can thus lead the respondent to underestimate or overestimate his own situation. This is particularly true in SMEs due to the personal and emotional involvement of the business owner. To reduce this subjectivity, the wording of the questions appears to be a key point and must be rigorously analyzed. The evaluation of the PE2I is based on the identification of observable phenomena. The tangible and verifiable nature of these phenomena is a means of limiting the subjectivity of the answers by encouraging a factual evaluation without value judgments. Thus, in view of the constitution of the PE2I evaluation reference system, self-evaluation seems to be a possible means of evolution of this tool to facilitate its large-scale dissemination. However, it is conditioned by the implementation of an adequate computer development allowing the hosting of the tool on an online platform and allowing the automatic visualization of the results of the evaluation and the associated recommendations.

5.2.2. *Contextualization of the recommendation system: taking into account differentiating factors*

This area of improvement consists of improving the adaptability of the diagnosis in order to integrate the context of each company into the evaluation, with the aim of proposing an evaluation that best reflects reality. At present, the diagnostic proposes a standardized evaluation of SMEs, with an undifferentiated reference framework of practices. One way to improve would be to introduce into this reference framework the taking into account of different factors, according to which it would be relevant to adapt the proposed evaluation. For example, the first tests carried out have shown that the sector of activity can potentially appear as a relevant differentiating factor, as the interpretation and implementation of certain practices vary from one sector to another. Similarly, the size of companies could also be a point of attention, as it potentially reflects a certain level of structuring that has a direct impact on the assessment proposed by the diagnosis. These non-exhaustive factors reveal potential specificities in the daily practices of SMEs in terms of innovation and exporting. The PE2I should therefore take a deeper look at these specificities from a contingent perspective in order to take them into account in its evaluation.

However, the PE2I is also based on an integrative logic that makes it possible to propose a standard indicator for evaluating the innovation and export capability of SMEs. A single indicator makes it possible to envisage comparative studies by sector or by region, or even within a panel of specific companies. This type of global comparison has already been carried out. For example, Galvez *et al.* (2013) propose a comparison of the innovation capacity of French and Argentine companies using the PII tool. The export and innovation capacity of Argentine SMEs has also been assessed by Desgens (2017) and Gili Vargas (2019) at the scale of the San Juan wine region. Finally, this standard indicator was used by Enjolras *et al.* (2019) to analyze the impact of technological intensity on SMEs' innovation and export capability. Thus, through the contextualization of the PE2I, it would not be wise to abandon its standardized nature. We, therefore, suggest integrating an opportunity for customization in the case where necessary, but without moving towards a case-by-case assessment. The tool could therefore take the form of a generic diagnosis, based on a fixed reference framework of practices, but customizable according to the relevant contingency factors adapted to each situation.

In practice, the contextualization of the tool can take several forms. The first option is to propose an individualized personalization of the proposed recommendations. It would be interesting to force the calculation of the progress plan by imposing certain conditions. For example, it could be relevant to freeze the calculation of recommendations on a particular practice if it is a topic on which the company cannot/would not act. The tool could then propose other recommendations, ignoring the frozen practice. In this way, a practice on which the company does not wish to act for strategic or operational reasons will still be evaluated but will not be included in the proposed recommendations. This solution has the advantage of preserving the general structure of the repository while offering the option of customizing it on a case-by-case basis. However, this customization remains limited.

In order to move towards a finer customization of the model, it could be envisaged to modify the structure of the practices repository so as to adapt it according to defined differentiating factors: addition or deletion of practices according to their relevance, rewording of the questions to adapt them to the jargon of the sector, modification of the maturity levels to smooth out the potential progression and so on. This type of modification has already been outlined through the research work of Desgens (2017), who proposed an update of the Potential Innovation Index (PII) to adapt it to wine SMEs in the San Juan region of Argentina. This adaptation leads, among other things, to the modification of the "design" practice in order to be more consistent with the functioning of wine companies. Indeed, innovation in the wine sector is mainly oriented towards processes and little towards the product. The design practice can therefore be approached a little differently.

This study also highlighted the need to include a new practice in the standard, reflecting a current concern of the sector: environmental responsibility. This solution offers interesting work perspectives, proposing a compromise between individual customization and standardization. However, it proposes to base the tool not on a single repository of standard practices but on a multitude of different combinations. This can pose significant operational problems and make the associated evaluation model significantly more cumbersome.

In order to maintain the standard structure of the tool, other options can be considered. Its construction logic, based on multi-criteria analysis methods, makes it possible, on the one hand, to propose a weighting of its repository of practices according to their importance, that is, according to their potential impact on innovation and export capabilities. Thus, depending on the weighting assigned to it, the evaluation of each practice does not make the same contribution to the overall evaluation of the company. By proposing a differentiated weighting that can be adapted to the sector of activity, for example, the PE2I would gain in flexibility in its evaluation while maintaining a reference framework of standard practices. However, the creation of differentiated weights requires a significant amount of testing in order to obtain statistically representative data for the differentiation factors considered.

On the contrary, the FlowSort method is used to aggregate the evaluations of each practice into a global indicator and to propose predefined categories in which to classify companies (passive, reactive, preactive and proactive with regard to innovation capacity; homebody, traveler, explorer and adventurer with regard to export capacity). These categories are defined by class profiles that make it possible to classify the evaluated company in the category that corresponds to its situation. Each category, therefore, has its own typical profile regarding the level of maturity of the practices assessed. In its current state of development, the tool relies on undifferentiated class profiles to categorize companies. However, it could be considered to modify the class boundaries of the innovation and export categories in order to customize them. For example, a company that is proactive in terms of innovation will potentially not have the same profile if it is from the agri-food sector or if it is from a high-tech sector. And this will potentially also be the case if we consider the export profile. Thus, if an agri-food company belongs to the proactive category in terms of innovation, another company from a high-tech sector with the same maturity profile could, for example, be classified in the lower (preactive) category because the sector of activity in which it evolves implies particularities that make it more demanding in terms of certain specific practices. For this, it is possible to rely on the work of Morel (2007), who experimented with the design of these class profiles, using fuzzy logic applied to an industrial sample of 20 companies. This research work has made it possible to identify membership functions, describing the characteristics of each category relating to innovation.

5.2.3. *Proposing evidence-based recommendations: an operational action plan to promote synergies*

This work perspective aims to go further in the recommendations proposed to companies following the diagnosis. In its current state, the prototype makes it possible to visualize the company's current profile and to identify priority areas for improvement based on the strengths and weaknesses detected by the tool. However, it does not allow for an operational action plan to be associated with it, and as far as possible, adapted to the context in which the company evolves, as well as to its specificities. However, this operational action plan should be a means of exploiting the synergies between innovation and exporting and of creating bridges between the practices to be improved. It should therefore propose joint recommendations, having a simultaneous impact in terms of innovation and export.

To achieve this joint and customizable operational action plan, the structuring of the tool according to maturity grids appears to be a valuable asset. During the assessment, the company is positioned on a level of each maturity grid corresponding to its situation for all the practices assessed. Thus, in order to improve its performance, the company must seek to raise the level of practices deemed critical to a higher level. For a given practice, the recommendations for improvement can therefore be based on the observable phenomena of the higher level. It is then possible to formulate concrete actions for companies, aiming at the appearance of tangible and reliable observable phenomena within their organization.

However, improving the innovation and export capabilities of companies does not necessarily mean pushing companies to improve all their practices. This action plan corresponds to a real strategic reflection led by the company. The choices can be multiple: Improve the weak points? Reinforce the strong points? Focus on innovation? Or export? Different improvement scenarios must be considered. Moreover, in the particular context of SMEs, the main difficulty is the lack of resources (Szczepanski 2016). Thus, the action plan to be proposed must be realistic and adapted to the company's resources.

For this, it is possible to act on two elements:

– optimization of resources to be mobilized to limit the investment to be made;

– hierarchy of actions to be implemented in order to propose a prioritization.

The exploitation of synergies between innovation and export thus appears to be an interesting lever in the optimization of resources to be mobilized. Indeed, by proposing joint innovation–export actions, it is possible, depending on the improvement scenario envisaged, to:

– Rely on an innovation driver to progress in export: for example, a company that masters the mobilization of a strong network of innovation partners could rely on this network to identify opportunities for international action.

– Rely on an export driver to progress in innovation: for example, a good understanding of international regulations and normative trends can be a valuable asset for anticipating new product developments and moving from a reactive to a proactive attitude.

– Work simultaneously on its innovation and export capabilities: for example, by considering the design process of a new product through a product–market pair, the human resources involved in this process acquire a joint mastery of the commercial and technical elements associated with this product, which encourages exchanges and brings out synergies in the daily functioning of the company.

The first two options aim to improve an activity from elements already mastered. This potentially requires no additional resources to be mobilized (or very few). It is a matter of optimizing existing resources. The last option, on the contrary, is oriented towards a joint performance increase. The company creates new internal routines, which simultaneously benefit its capacity for innovation and export, and mobilizes resources dedicated to this rise in competence.

Regarding the prioritization of actions to be implemented, it is currently done on the basis of the difference between the score of each practice (weighted according to its importance) and the overall PE2I score. The greater the difference, the more negative the impact of the practice on the overall index. The objective is to focus on practices that are considered critical, which correspond to weak points. Thus, depending on the improvement scenario chosen (export-oriented or innovation-oriented, for example), the practices are weighted differently and, therefore, the criticality calculation is also different. The weak points of one scenario are not necessarily the weak points of another. This prioritization works relatively well in the current state of development of the tool. However, it could be interesting to add additional factors. For example, this prioritization could be based on a cost–benefit ratio. An experiment in this direction was initiated in the work of Galvez (2015). Through the respective use of an optimization algorithm and a planning algorithm, the objective was to identify, according to different scenarios, the priority recommendations to be proposed to improve the innovation capacity of companies: how to identify the innovation practices to be improved and how to sequence the improvement actions to achieve the greatest impact, while limiting the associated resources. Thus, based on several defined factors, the creation of a prioritization algorithm is a way forward to improve PE2I.

Conclusion

The scientific position that we defend through this work consists of considering innovation and export in SMEs as two complementary activities integrating a common space. This common space represents the activities/resources/skills that an SME must mobilize as a priority in order to simultaneously improve its performance in terms of innovation and export while reducing the effort associated with this increase in performance. Thus, this research work leads to the identification of this common innovation–export space, to its characterization in terms of joint activities and finally, to its exploitation through the creation of a tool to support SMEs, encouraging them to act in priority on this common space.

C.1. The contributions

This book proposes various contributions relating to several scientific fields linked to the study of SMEs' innovation and export capabilities. Part 1 (Chapters 1 and 2), which is more theoretical, aims at building a relevant analytical framework to address the issue of innovation and export in SMEs. Part 2 (Chapters 3 and 4), which is more operational, aims to design and test an evaluation tool to implement a complex vision of the innovation–export relationship in support of SMEs.

More precisely, the objective of Chapter 1 is to present the scientific position chosen for this research work. By analyzing the innovation–export relationship, on the one hand, through the prism of scientific research, and on the other hand, through the actions put in place in a concrete way for the support proposed to SMEs, we have put forward the limits and stakes of this field of research.

The link between innovation and export is mostly considered under the influence of a causal paradigm. However, the relationship between innovation and export is not limited to a cause-and-effect relationship (Golovko and Valentini 2011). From an operational point of view, an international benchmarking of export support systems has also made it possible to highlight the compartmentalization of the support offered to SMEs. Innovation and export are generally treated separately both within companies and by the support organizations concerned.

The main contribution of Chapter 1 is, therefore, to propose a new vision of the innovation–export relationship through the complexity paradigm, which allows us to propose an alternative to the current compartmentalized causal vision. Through this chapter, we encourage the operational implementation of joint innovation–export support. This chapter represents an important contribution to the improvement of the support offered by business support organizations.

To do so, we rely on the articulation of different scientific theories related to our problematic, in order to propose a solid theoretical framework adapted to our research context: innovative and exporting SMEs. By combining the contributions of the SCP (structure, conduct and performance) model of industrial economics theory with those of contingency theory, resource-based view and RARe (resources, activities and results) models, this chapter has allowed us to present a revisited SCP model that is adapted to our research work. We thus bring together several fields of research specific to both management sciences and industrial engineering in order to propose a global vision of the problem of innovation and export in SMEs.

In keeping with the scientific position established in Chapter 1, we then make the hypothesis in Chapter 2 that innovation and export can be considered as two separate spaces but with a common interface. The objective of this chapter is to characterize the innovation and export spaces, respectively, through the identification of good practices so as to better link them later to characterize a common innovation–export space.

Based on the Potential Innovation Index (PII) of the ERPI laboratory of the University of Lorraine (Boly *et al.* 2000), we propose a characterization of the innovation space in the form of a structure with three levels of aggregation: practices/activities/observable phenomena. Within this structure, each practice and each activity is weighted according to the strength of its impact on the innovation capability of companies. By analogy, we have proposed a similar structure to characterize the export space through the creation of the Potential Export Index (PEI) to evaluate the export capability of SMEs.

The PEI and PII are based on a particular evaluation principle. The aim is to evaluate the potential capability of a company to export (or to innovate for the PII). The evaluation of companies is therefore not based on financial or other performance indicators. It is a question of measuring the degree of mastery of the companies concerning the essential activities that must be carried out in order to export (or innovate). Thus, these tools do not evaluate whether the company is exporting (innovating) correctly; they measure whether it is capable, potentially, of doing so. Here again, this is an important contribution both from a scientific point of view and from the point of view of public authorities or SME support organizations. To enable companies to engage in export or innovation activities, it is not enough to encourage them to do so with punctual support aimed at increasing their temporary resources (although access to resources is the main difficulty for these small structures). Instead, it is necessary to ensure that they are capable of carrying out and managing these activities, that is, that they master the best practices for creating favorable conditions for the sustainability of the actions implemented.

After having characterized the innovation and export spaces separately, the aim is to combine innovation and export activities within a single common space. Thanks to a similarity analysis and a spatialization of data, the common innovation–export space was identified and characterized in two steps. First, the activities common to both spaces were identified and their degree of similarity was assessed. Then, these common activities were combined in order to bring out joint activities through a spatialization of data. Thus, the contribution of Chapter 3 lies in the identification and characterization of the common innovation–export space through joint practices acting simultaneously on the innovation and export capabilities in the form of synergies. The theoretical results of the analysis of similarities have been confronted with the reality of the business world through different case studies, which have allowed us to observe these synergistic effects and to attest to their relevance. This chapter represents a validation of our scientific position: the common innovation–export space does exist, and it represents a very important part of the innovation and export spaces. This chapter thus justifies the importance of considering innovation and export together, and this has very strong implications for support to SMEs.

Chapter 3 presents the operational development of the tool for evaluating the innovation and export capabilities: the PE2I (Potential Export and Innovation Index). The aim is to design a tool for SMEs focused on the evaluation of joint innovation and export activities, highlighting the potential capability of companies to innovate and export. This tool is based on the same principle as its founding elements (the PII and the PEI): it measures the degree of mastery of the practices considered and proposes recommendations for improvement. The contribution of this chapter, therefore, concerns the development of this tool: creation of a structure with three levels of aggregation, weighting of joint innovation–export activities according to their importance, creation of an automated mathematical system making it possible to obtain the profile of a company concerning its innovation and export capability, and creation of a system of recommendations that can be customized according to the company's strategy.

The PE2I was then tested (Chapter 4) in six French SMEs from various business sectors and of different sizes. The second contribution of this chapter is, therefore, to confront the evaluation tool with the vision of company managers in order to test it in real conditions with a mixed field of application: manufacturing and process SMEs. Feedback (Chapter 5) from these six case studies has highlighted the potential benefits of such a tool for companies, as well as the limitations associated with it, which still need to be worked on.

Thus, this research work has made it possible to provide several contributions to the problem of innovation and export within manufacturing and process SMEs. From the point of view of scientific research, the various contributions touch on:

– the proposal of a new vision of the innovation–export relationship: not in terms of the impact of one on the other, but in terms of complementarities;

– the application of the complexity paradigm to innovation and export in SMEs;

– the identification and characterization of a common innovation–export space in the form of joint practices.

From the point of view of managerial and institutional implications, the creation and application of a tool to evaluate the innovation and export capabilities have made it possible to bring to the forefront various observations to which we are trying to provide a solution through this research work:

– support for SMEs is mainly oriented towards raising awareness and providing one-off financing, particularly in the case of exports. However, it is necessary to accompany companies in the modification and structuring of their internal processes in order to enable them to face the difficulties they will encounter. An evaluation tool to measure their degree of mastery of the activities essential to innovation and export makes sense;

– innovation support and export support are generally provided by different institutional actors and are often mobilized by separate departments within companies. However, we have highlighted the significant size of the common space between innovation and export, as well as the benefits of coupling export and innovation support systems for SMEs. By exploiting the relationship between innovation and export in the support offered to companies, we can move from a compartmentalized and specific support to an integrative and complex support by creating links and interdepartmental exchanges;

– within SMEs, access to resources is generally difficult. Focusing on the common innovation–export space allows SMEs to develop joint activities. It is a question of activating a single lever, which has an impact on both the innovation and export capabilities. By seeking to promote actions that lead to the emergence of synergies, we maximize the potential impact on SMEs' innovation and export capability. Acting on the common space reduces the effort associated with increasing the performance of companies and optimizes the allocation of resources.

Thus, the contributions of this research work concern both the scientific research and the business world. The results obtained are promising, and they open interesting research perspectives to continue in this way.

C.2. Limitations

As in any research work, certain limitations can be considered in order to qualify certain results. The first limitation of our research work concerns the implementation of the PE2I. We proceeded by case studies with six manufacturing and process SMEs. We opted for a qualitative validation methodology, and the results obtained are promising in both the manufacturing and process sectors. However, in order to judge the relevance of the tool from a general point of view, it seems necessary to test it with a larger number of SMEs, from different sectors of activity and with varying numbers of employees. A quantitative validation would indeed bring robustness to the PE2I, allowing to confirm or deny the trends identified during the first test phase.

A second limitation of this study concerns the operational development of the tool. It was decided to propose a semi-automated evaluation tool. However, it is essential that this tool remains customizable. The various tests of the tool in real-life situations have enabled us to highlight the great disparities within the SMEs evaluated. It is indeed essential to take into account the heterogeneity of the companies, and this heterogeneity is not only linked to a difference of activity sector or size. Each company is different; there is no "standard" structure (Mintzberg 1979), and this is particularly true in the case of SMEs. By choosing to develop a semi-automated assessment tool, customization is necessarily limited. This limitation was particularly noticeable when creating the progress plan for the companies evaluated. On a case-by-case basis, certain dimensions were more or less important to the company. On the contrary, the tool is based on the bias of denaturing SMEs (Torrès and Julien 2005), according to which innovation and exporting force companies to implement more formalized management of their internal processes. The recommendations proposed to companies were therefore intended to encourage the formalization and structuring of their activities. Here again, depending on the context of each evaluation, the choice of formalization as the main recommendation was not always the most appropriate. The question of the tool's adaptability is therefore raised. It is necessary to find a compromise between personalization and standardization in order to be in line with the particular functioning of these small structures and to best meet the needs of SME managers.

Finally, the main limitation of our work concerns the point of view chosen to study SMEs. We have chosen to focus on internal processes, and therefore on the activities implemented by the companies from an organizational point of view. However, a very important part of the literature on SMEs is dedicated to the place of the manager within these small structures. In general, human aspects play an extremely important role in innovation (Rodriguez and Hechanova 2014) and export activities (Alaoui and Makrini 2014). This is even more true in the context of SMEs, as the leader is omnipresent and sometimes the sole decision-maker (Child and Hsieh 2014). The profile of the leader remains an extremely important point to take into account when assessing the innovation and export capabilities of SMEs. Yet, although some studies are devoted to it (Pettersen *et al.* 2011), it is extremely difficult to assess the profile of an SME leader in the form of verifiable and quantifiable indicators. Moreover, it seems difficult to characterize the profile of the leader in the form of observable activities and phenomena. Hence, this human dimension has not been integrated into this study. However, the study of the leader's profile opens an interesting research perspective. The personality of a manager cannot be considered as a necessary activity to improve the innovation and export capabilities of an SME, but it can be considered as a resource or a facilitator. Indeed, we place ourselves in a theoretical framework based on a triptych resource-activity-result. Thus, each activity leads to a result, but it is dependent on the resources available. The implementation of joint innovation and export activities is therefore strongly dependent on the presence or absence of the necessary resources. These resources, joint to innovation and export, are therefore an element limiting the potential improvement of the innovation and export capability of SMEs. From this point of view, it seems quite appropriate to consider the profile of the manager as a joint resource that needs to be exploited. Our research work is limited to the study of joint activities. The analysis of joint resources for innovation and export also seems to be an interesting research perspective.

C.3. To go further

Thus, these first results pave the way to several research perspectives. These avenues for improvement are first theoretical, through the consolidation of the characterization of the common innovation–export space. They are also operational through the further development of the PE2I.

C.3.1. *Strengthening the characterization of the common innovation–export space*

As mentioned, one of the main limitations of this study is the choice to focus on joint innovation–export activities to characterize the common space. This choice was made because innovation and exporting push companies to modify their internal processes so as to face the difficulties linked, for example, to the penetration of a new market or the introduction of a new technology. In order to manage the changes introduced by innovation and export, companies need to mobilize specific resources and exploit them through adapted activities. Currently, PE2I offers SMEs a diagnosis of their degree of mastery of joint innovation–export activities. The objective of this tool is to assess whether they are potentially capable of identifying and exploiting the resources they need to carry out their innovation and export activities simultaneously. Our analysis is therefore situated at the level of activities, which are implicitly dependent on the resources available, but which are also a guarantee of their proper exploitation. In order to be efficiently used, a resource must be exploited through a specific activity, but this activity is only possible if the necessary resources are made available. Resources and activities are dependent on each other. It, therefore, seems interesting to go down the analysis to the level of resources in order to propose a finer characterization of the common innovation–export space.

Based on this observation, we propose to identify two types of resources:

– consumable resources: these are resources that the company can acquire or enrich according to its needs. Typically, a new supplier, more efficient technical equipment or additional skills are consumable resources that the company needs to implement its innovation and export process. It is these resources that the company exploits by setting up specific activities;

– moderating resources: these are resources that the company cannot influence directly. These resources are not substitutable; they are limiting. For example, the profile of the manager and his or her behavior in the face of risk-taking appear to be a moderating resource. It conditions the change in the company's internal processes.

These two types of resources impact the evaluation of the innovation and export capability in two different ways. First, it seems possible to associate, with each joint innovation–export activity, a certain number of consumable resources that are necessary for the implementation of the activity in question. We, therefore, propose to identify the joint innovation–export resources, which, associated with the joint activities identified in this research work, would bring an additional degree of precision to the characterization of the joint innovation–export space. The identification of these joint consumable resources would also be an important contribution to proposing relevant and realistic recommendations to SMEs. The PE2I evaluation suggests that the company should improve its "information acquisition" activity. What are the resources to be mobilized for this activity? Are they easily accessible and mobilizable? The effort associated with improving the "information acquisition" activity can thus be estimated according to the difficulty of accessing the necessary consumable resources. The use of RARe models (Boly 2008) could represent an interesting contribution to this study. According to these models, four operations can be performed on resources (Ben Rejeb 2008):

– addition: introduction of a new resource;

– substitution: replacement of an existing resource by another;

– improvement: consolidation of an existing resource;

– integration: merging several resources into one.

The implementation or improvement of an activity potentially requires one or more of these operations to be performed regarding the company's resources. The identification of the type of operation to be performed can also be an indicator of the effort required to improve an activity.

As for the joint innovation–export moderating resources, they can potentially have a strong impact on the innovation and export capabilities. They can appear as success or failure factors that should not be neglected. Currently, the PE2I proposes an evaluation of the potential innovation and export capability of SMEs. The study of these moderating resources could make it possible to nuance this potential capability in order to get closer to a real and contextualized capability.

The analysis of the manager's profile seems to be a relevant example of a joint moderating resource. An SME may indeed demonstrate innovation and export capability with significant potential, but the attitude of its manager towards risk-taking, for example, may slow down or even block its international development and/or its innovation approach. The first step in the study of joint moderating resources could be to propose an evaluation of the SME manager's profile. This evaluation would follow the evaluation of the potential innovation and export capability of SMEs (via the PE2I) in order to nuance the results obtained and to contextualize them. The behavior of SME managers is an important research topic (Jaouen and Lasch 2013; Chabaud and Sammut 2016). However, the proposed work generally faces methodological difficulties. Indeed, the assessment of managers' behaviors is generally carried out in the form of self-diagnosis, which introduces a certain bias. However, Pettersen *et al.* (2011) propose a multi-source assessment tool to provide a more objective assessment. This tool could be an interesting basis for investigating this field of research.

C.3.2. *Taking the operational development of the tool further*

The second perspective of this research work concerns the operational development of the PE2I. Currently, the tool works semi-automatically, but its adaptability is limited. However, we noted in Chapter 5 that it was necessary for PE2I to adapt to particular cases in view of the heterogeneity of SMEs. The first step in improving the tool is, therefore, to find a compromise between standardization and customization.

To do this, it is first necessary to continue testing the PE2I on a larger number of SMEs, both manufacturing and process. Ideally, we would like to build a representative panel of SMEs of all sizes and from various sectors of activity so as to propose quantitative observations. During the tests, we were able to observe that, depending on the case, the importance given to the nine joint innovation–export dimensions evaluated was different. Some dimensions were even considered irrelevant in some cases. The data collected would make it possible to obtain indications of these variations, depending on the context of the SMEs considered: Does the importance of the dimensions change according to the sector of activity, the size, the age and the environment? A quantitative analysis would make it possible to identify typical profiles and to propose different weightings adapted to these profiles.

In the same way, we observed that the recommendations proposed by the PE2I in the case of small companies were not always relevant. These recommendations are based on a dynamic of structuring and formalization, which does not always make sense in smaller structures.

Thus, a quantitative analysis would also make it possible to observe whether this lack of relevance of formalization is indeed linked to the size factor or whether it depends on other elements. A data analysis would also make it possible to set thresholds for limiting recommendations according to the size of the company if this proves relevant. These different parameters concerning the weighting of the dimensions or the formalization threshold would make the PE2I more flexible and more easily customizable.

In the longer term, it would also be possible to extend the tests to different geographical areas in order to identify possible cultural differences. A thorough quantitative analysis would therefore make it possible to identify disparities, particularly in terms of size, sectors of activity and geographical areas. The results of such a quantitative study could be integrated into a database, the exploitation of which would represent an opportunity to increase scientific knowledge on SMEs at the regional, national and international levels.

The data collected from the companies can be analyzed using clustering methods, principal component analysis (PCA), rough set theory and so on, in order to identify typical profiles that constitute a taxonomy of innovative and exporting SMEs. From this taxonomy, it will be possible to identify ways to improve the tool (precision of the categories, improvement of the proposed recommendations, etc.). In addition, this taxonomy would also make it possible to identify the guidelines to be considered in terms of personalized support for SMEs according to their context. Sectoral and/or regional benchmarking could thus be carried out in order to provide factual data to the institutions concerned to better target their support initiatives.

Thus, the PE2I brings a contribution thanks to its complex vision of the innovation–export relationship and thanks to the principle of its evaluation, based on a measurement of potential rather than on a measurement of performance. These different perspectives of research, both theoretical and operational, open the way to interesting contributions nourishing the ambition to go towards the proposal of a joint innovation/export support offer, relevant and adaptable to the heterogeneous and particular context of SMEs.

References

Abedi, M., Ali Torabi, S., Norouzi, G.-H., Hamzeh, M., Elyasi, G.-R. (2012). PROMETHEE II: A knowledge-driven method for copper exploration. *Computers & Geosciences*, 46, 255–263.

Adams, R., Bessant, J., Phelps, R. (2006). Innovation management measurement: A review. *International Journal of Management Reviews*, 8, 21–47.

Akinwale, Y.O., Akinbami, J.F.K., Akarakiri, J.B. (2018). Factors influencing technology and innovation capability in the Nigerian indigenous oil firms. *International Journal of Business Innovation and Research*, 15, 247–268.

Alaoui, A. and Makrini, H.E. (2014). Analyse des effets des pratiques managériales sur la performance à l'export. Étude empirique des PME marocaines. *Revue management & avenir*, 72, 15–33.

Albadvi, A., Chaharsooghi, S.K., Esfahanipour, A. (2007). Decision-making in stock trading: An application of PROMETHEE. *European Journal of Operational Research*, 177, 673–683.

Altomonte, C., Aquilante, T., Békés, G., Ottaviano, G.P. (2013). Internationalization and innovation of firms: Evidence and policy. *Economic Policy*, 28, 663–700.

Andersen, E.S. and Jessen, S.A. (2003). Project maturity in organisations. *International Journal of Project Management*, 21, 457–461.

Anil, N.K. and Shoham, A. (2017). Testing an integrative model of export performance in Turkish SMEs. In *Proceedings of the Academy of Marketing Science*, Campbell, C.R. (ed.). Springer, Cham.

Antunes, P., Carreira, P., Mira da Silva, M. (2014). Towards an energy management maturity model. *Energy Policy*, 73, 803–814.

Ayllon, S. and Radicic, D. (2019). Product innovation, process innovation and export propensity: Persistence, complementarities and feedback effects in Spanish firms. *Applied Economics*, 51, 3650–3664.

Bain, J.S. (1968). *Industrial Organization*. John Wiley & Sons, Hoboken, NJ.

Barney, J. (1991). Firm resources and sustained competitive advantage. *Journal of Management*, 17, 99–120.

Becker, S.O. and Egger, P.H. (2013). Endogenous product versus process innovation and a firm's propensity to export. *Empirical Economics*, 44, 329–354.

Belas, J., Ivanova, E., Rozsa, Z., Schonfeld, J. (2018). Innovations in SME segment: Important factors and differences in the approach by size and age of the company. *Transformations in Business & Economics*, 17, 55–71.

Bellone, F. and Guillou, S. (2013). Innovation et primes à l'exportation : une analyse empirique sur données d'entreprises françaises. *Économie & prévision*, 197/198, 45–61.

Ben Rejeb, H. (2008). Phases amont de l'innovation : proposition d'une démarche d'analyse de besoin et d'évaluation de l'acceptabilité d'un produit. PhD Thesis, Institut National Polytechnique de Lorraine, Vandœuvre-lès-Nancy.

Ben Rejeb, H., Morel-Guimarães, L., Boly, V., Assiélou, N.G. (2008). Measuring innovation best practices: Improvement of an innovation index integrating threshold and synergy effects. *Technovation*, 28, 838–854.

Berrah, L. (2013). La quantification de la performance dans les entreprises manufacturières : de la déclaration des objectifs à la définition des systèmes d'indicateurs. HDR Thesis (HDR) – Speciality in Sciences and Information and Communication Sciences, Université de Savoie, Chambéry.

van Beveren, I. and Vandenbussche, H. (2010). Product and process innovation and firms' decision to export. *Journal of Economic Policy Reform*, 13, 3–24.

Bianchi, C. and Wickramasekera, R. (2016). Antecedents of SME export intensity in a Latin American market. *Journal of Business Research*, 69(10), 4368–4376.

Blackstone, J.H. and Cox, J.F. (1985). Are small manufacturers ready for MRP? *Comptes rendus de la 27ème conférence internationale annuelle de l'APICS*, 3–6.

Blondel, V.D., Guillaume, J.-L., Lambiotte, R., Lefebvre, E. (2008). Fast unfolding of communities in large network. *Journal of Statistical Mechanics*, P10008, 1–12.

Bołkunow, W. (2019). Internationalization of European small and medium-sized companies. In *Eurasian Business Perspectives, Eurasian Studies in Business and Economics*, Bilgin, M.H., Danis, H., Demir, E., Can, U. (eds). Springer, Cham.

Boly, V. (2004). *Ingénierie de l'innovation : organisation et méthodologies des entreprises innovantes*. Hermes-Lavoisier, Paris.

Boly, V. (2008). *Ingénierie de l'innovation : organisation et méthodologies des entreprises innovantes*, 2nd edition. Hermes-Lavoisier, Paris.

Boly, V., Morel, L., Renaud, J., Guidat, C. (2000). Innovation in low tech SMBs: Evidence of a necessary constructivist approach. *Technovation*, 20, 161–168.

Boly, V., Morel, L., Assielou, N.G., Camargo, M. (2014). Evaluating innovative processes in French firms: Methodological proposition for firm innovation capacity evaluation. *Research Policy*, 43, 608–622.

Boso, N., Story, V.M., Cadogan, J.W., Micevski, M., Kadić-Maglajlić, S. (2013). Firm innovativeness and export performance: Environmental, networking, and structural contingencies. *Journal of International Marketing*, 21, 62–87.

Boutary, M., Faure, R., Monnoyer, M.-C. (2013). PME et groupements : antinomie définitive ou nouvelle nécessité ? *Revue des sciences de gestion*, 101–109.

BPI France (2011a). Rapport sur l'évolution des PME. Banque Publique d'Investissement France, Observatoire des PME.

BPI France (2011b). La défaillance des entreprises, étude sur données françaises entre 2000 et 2010. Observatoire des PME.

Brulhart, F., Guieu, G., Maltese, L. (2010). Théorie des ressources. *Revue française de gestion*, 204, 83–86.

Caldera, A. (2010). Innovation and exporting: Evidence from Spanish manufacturing firms. *Review of World Economics*, 146, 657–689.

Calori, R., Very, P., Arregle, J.-L. (1997). Les PMI face à la planification stratégique. *Revue française de gestion*, 112, 11–23.

Cassiman, B. and Golovko, E. (2011). Innovation and internationalization through exports. *Journal of International Business Studies*, 42, 56–75.

Cassiman, B., Golovko, E., Martínez-Ros, E. (2010). Innovation, exports and productivity. *International Journal of Industrial Organization*, 28, 372–376.

Catanzaro, A., Messeghem, K., Sammut, S. (2013). Accompagner l'entreprise à internationalisation précoce et rapide : la place centrale de la dimension réticulaire. *Revue de l'entrepreneuriat*, 11, 33–53.

Chabaud, D. and Sammut, S. (2016). Le dirigeant au cœur des dynamiques entrepreneuriales des PME. *Revue de l'entrepreneuriat*, 15, 7–13.

Chen, T., Chen, X., Wang, C., Xiang, X. (2018). Export behavior and firm innovation: New method and evidence. *Economics Letters*, 170, 76–78.

Chesbrough, H. (2003). The logic of open innovation: Managing intellectual property. *California Management Review*, 45, 33–58.

Chiesa, V., Coughlan, P., Voss, C.A. (1996). Development of a technical innovation audit. *Journal of Product Innovation Management*, 13, 105–136.

Child, J. and Hsieh, L.H.Y. (2014). Decision mode, information and network attachment in the internationalization of SMEs: A configurational and contingency analysis. *Journal of World Business*, 49, 598–610.

Choi, Y.S. and Lim, U. (2017). Contextual factors affecting the innovation performance of manufacturing SMEs in Korea: A structural equation modeling approach. *Sustainability*, 9(7), 1193.

Cinelli, M., Coles, S.R., Kirwan, K. (2014). Analysis of the potentials of multi criteria decision analysis methods to conduct sustainability assessment. *Ecological Indicators*, 46, 138–148.

Cleveland, W.S. (1993). *Visualizing Data*. Hobart Press, Summit, NJ.

Collis, D. and Montgomery, C. (1995). Competing on resources: Strategy in the 1990s. *Harvard Business Review*, 73, 118–128.

Corona, J. (2005). Innovation et métrologie : une approche en termes d'indice d'innovation potentielle. PhD Thesis, Institut National Polytechnique de Lorraine, Nancy.

Crowley, F. and Jordan, D. (2017). Does more competition increase business-level innovation? Evidence from domestically focused firms in emerging economies. *Economics of Innovation and New Technology*, 26, 477–488.

Dai, M., Liu, H., Lin, L. (2019). How innovation impacts firms' export survival: Does export mode matter? *The World Economy*, 43(1), 81–113.

Damijan, J.P. and Kostevc, C. (2010). Learning from trade through innovation: Causal link between imports, exports and innovation in Spanish microdata. LICOS Discussion Paper, 264.

Damijan, J., Kostevc, C., Polanec, S. (2010). From innovation to exporting or vice versa? *The World Economy*, 33, 374–398.

De Rosnay, J. (1975). *Le macroscope : vers une vision globale*. Points, Paris.

Degenne, A. and Vergès, P. (1973). Introduction à l'analyse de similitude. *Revue française de sociologie*, 14, 471–512.

Deng, Z., Guo, H., Zhang, W., Wang, C. (2014). Innovation and survival of exporters: A contingency perspective. *International Business Review*, 23, 396–406.

Descartes, R. (1637). *Discours de la méthode*. Flammarion, Paris.

Desgens, L. (2017). Proposition d'adaptation de la capacité à innover dans un groupe de PME de la région de San Juan appartenant au secteur industriel vitivinicole. Master's Thesis, Université de Lorraine, Nancy.

Dhanaraj, C. and Beamish, P.W. (2003). A resource-based approach to the study of export performance. *Journal of Small Business Management*, 3, 242–261.

Di Cintio, M., Ghosh, S., Grassi, E. (2019). Direct or indirect exports: What matters for firms' innovation activities? *Applied Economics Letters*, 27(2), 93–103.

Diamantopoulos, A., Schlegelmilch, B.B., Katy Tse, K.Y. (1993). Understanding the role of export marketing assistance: Empirical evidence and research needs. *European Journal of Marketing*, 27, 5–18.

DiPietro, W.R. and Anoruo, E. (2006). Creativity, innovation, and export performance. *Journal of Policy Modeling*, 28, 133–139.

Durand, D. (2006). *La systémique*, 10th edition. PUF, Paris.

Edison, H., Bin Ali, N., Torkar, R. (2013). Towards innovation measurement in the software industry. *Journal of Systems and Software*, 86, 1390–1407.

Eggers, F., Niemand, T., Filser, M., Kraus, S., Berchtold, J. (2018). To network or not to network – Is that really the question? The impact of networking intensity and strategic orientations on innovation success. *Technological Forecasting and Social Change*, 155, 119448.

Eisenhardt, K.M. (1991). Better stories and better constructs: The case for rigor and comparative logic. *The Academy of Management Review*, 16, 620–627.

Enjolras, M. (2016). Méthodologie d'analyse de la capacité à innover et à exporter des PME manufacturières et de procédés : identification et caractérisation d'un espace commun en vue de l'élaboration d'un outil multicritères d'aide à la décision. PhD Thesis, Université de Lorraine, Nancy.

Enjolras, M., Camargo, M., Schmitt, C., Morel, L. (2015). Comparatif des dispositifs de soutien à l'internationalisation des PME : les apports de la prise en compte de l'innovation. *6ème rencontre du groupe de recherche thématique "innovation" de l'AIMS*. Strasbourg.

Enjolras, M., Camargo, M., Schmitt, C. (2016). SMEs' innovation and export capabilities: Identification and characterization of a common space using data spatialization. *Journal of Technology Management & Innovation*, 11, 56–69.

Enjolras, M., Camargo, M., Schmitt, C. (2019). Are high-tech companies more competitive than others? An empirical study of innovative and exporting French SMEs. *Technology Innovation Management Review*, 9, 33–48.

Etemad, H. (2004). Internationalization of small and medium-sized enterprises: A grounded theoretical framework and an overview. *Canadian Journal of Administrative Sciences*, 21, 1–21.

European Commission (2007). Supporting the internationalisation of SMEs (Final Report of the Expert Group). Report, Entrepreneurship Unit, Directorate-General for Enterprise and Industry.

European Commission (2016a). Annual Report on European SMEs 2015/2016. Report, European Commission.

European Commission (2016b). Support to SMEs, increasing research and innovation in SMEs and SME development: Ex post evaluation of Cohesion Policy programs 2007–2013, focusing on the European Regional Development Fund (ERDF) and the Cohesion Fund (CF): Executive summaries: Work package 2. Report, Directorate-General for Regional and Urban Policy.

European Commission (2016c). Guide de l'utilisateur pour la définition des PME, marché intérieur, industrie, entrepreneuriat et PME. Guide, European Commission.

European Commission (2018). Annual report on European SMEs 2017/2018: Special background document on the internationalisation of SMEs (SME Performance Review 2017/2018). Report, European Commission.

Fassio, C. (2018). Export-led innovation: The role of export destinations. *Industrial and Corporate Change*, 27, 149–171.

FedEx (2015). Export/import trends and behaviours of SMEs in Europe. European SME Export Report, FedEx.

Filatotchev, I. and Piesse, J. (2009). R&D, internationalization and growth of newly listed firms: European evidence. *Journal of International Business Studies*, 40, 1260–1276.

Filipescu, D.A., Prashantham, S., Rialp, A., Rialp, J. (2013). Technological innovation and exports: Unpacking their reciprocal causality. *Journal of International Marketing*, 21, 23–38.

Forés, B. and Camisón, C. (2016). Does incremental and radical innovation performance depend on different types of knowledge accumulation capabilities and organizational size? *Journal of Business Research*, 69, 831–848.

Forsman, H. (2011). Innovation capacity and innovation development in small enterprises. A comparison between the manufacturing and service sectors. *Research Policy*, 40, 739–750.

Francis, J. and Collins-Dodd, C. (2004). Impact of export promotion programs on firm competencies, strategies and performance: The case of Canadian high-technology SMEs. *International Marketing Review*, 21, 474–495.

Fruchterman, T.M.J. and Reingold, E.M. (1991). Graph drawing by force-directed placement. *Software: Practice and Experience*, 21, 1129–1164.

Galvez, D. (2015). Évaluation de la capacité à innover : une approche par auto-évaluation et suivi supporté par des analyses multicritères dynamiques. PhD Thesis, Université de Lorraine, Nancy.

Galvez, D., Camargo, M., Rodriguez, J., Morel, L. (2013). PII potential innovation index: A tool to benchmark innovation capabilities in international context. *Journal of Technology Management & Innovation*, 8, 36–45.

García Pérez de Lema, D., Trejo, V.G.S., Bárcenas, R.E. (2012). Facteurs caractéristiques de la planification stratégique dans la PMI : une étude empirique sur des entreprises en Espagne. *Recherches en sciences de gestion*, 19–33.

Gili Vargas, S. (2019). Le challenge de l'exportation en PME : le cas des entreprises vitivinicoles argentines. Master's Thesis, Université de Lorraine, ERPI, ENSGSI, Nancy.

Gkypali, A., Arvanitis, S., Tsekouras, K. (2018). Absorptive capacity, exporting activities, innovation openness and innovation performance: A SEM approach towards a unifying framework. *Technological Forecasting and Social Change*, 132, 143–155.

Glaser, B.G. and Strauss, A.L. (1968). *The Discovery of Grounded Theory: Strategies for Qualitative Research*. Aldine Transaction, New Brunswick/London.

Godet, M. (1997). *Manuel de prospective stratégique*. Dunod, Paris.

Golovko, E. and Valentini, G. (2011). Exploring the complementarity between innovation and export for SMEs growth. *Journal of International Business Studies*, 42, 362–380.

Golovko, E. and Valentini, G. (2014). Selective learning-by-exporting: Firm size and product versus process innovation. *Global Strategy Journal*, 4, 161–180.

Goy, H. and Paturel, R. (2004). Les problématiques de diagnostic et de projection dans les PMI. *Revue française de gestion*, 150, 55–70.

Guan, J.C., Yam, R.C.M., Mok, C.K., Ma, N. (2006). A study of the relationship between competitiveness and technological innovation capability based on DEA models. *European Journal of Operational Research*, 170, 971–986.

Guitouni, A. and Martel, J.-M. (1998). Tentative guidelines to help choosing an appropriate MCDA method. *European Journal of Operational Research*, 109, 501–521.

Hagedoorn, J. and Cloodt, M. (2003). Measuring innovative performance: Is there an advantage in using multiple indicators? *Research Policy*, 32, 1365–1379.

Halilem, N., Amara, N., Landry, R. (2014). Exploring the relationships between innovation and internationalization of small and medium-sized enterprises: A nonrecursive structural equation model. *Canadian Journal of Administrative Sciences*, 31, 18–34.

Hanel, P. (2006). Intellectual property rights business management practices: A survey of the literature. *Technovation*, 26, 895–931.

Hatzichronoglou, T. (1997). Révision des classifications des secteurs et produits de haute technologie. OCDE/GD report, (97)216. DSTI working documents (Direction de la Science, de la Technologie et de l'Industrie).

van den Heiligenberg, H.A.R.M., Heimeriks, G.J., Hekkert, M.P., Van Oort, F.G. (2017). A habitat for sustainability experiments: Success factors for innovations in their local and regional contexts. *Journal of Cleaner Production*, 169, 204–215.

Higón, D.A. and Driffield, N. (2011). Exporting and innovation performance: Analysis of the annual small business survey in the UK. *International Small Business Journal*, 29, 4–24.

Hlady-Rispal, M. (2016). Une stratégie de recherche en gestion. *Revue française de gestion*, 251–266.

Hohenthal, J., Johanson, J., Johanson, M. (2014). Network knowledge and business-relationship value in the foreign market. *International Business Review*, 23, 4–19.

Hughes, A. and Mina, A. (2010). The impact of the patent system on SMEs. Working paper, 411, University of Cambridge, Centre for Business Research.

Ishizaka, A. and Nemery, P. (2011). Selecting the best statistical distribution with PROMETHEE and GAIA. *Computers & Industrial Engineering*, 61, 958–969.

Ishizaka, A. and Nemery, P. (2013). *Multi-criteria Decision Analysis: Methods and Software*. Wiley-Blackwell, Chichester.

ISO (2019). ISO 56002: 2019. Innovation management – Innovation management system – Guidance. ISO, Geneva.

Jacomy, M., Heymann, S., Venturini, T., Bastian, M. (2014). ForceAtlas2: A graph layout algorithm for handy network visualization design for the Gephi software. *PLoS ONE*, 9(6), e98679.

Jaouen, A. and Lasch, F. (2013). A new typology of micro-firm owner-managers. *International Small Business Journal*, 33(4), 397–421.

Julien, P.-A. (2005). *Entrepreneuriat régional et économie de la connaissance*. Presses de l'Université du Québec, Montreal.

Kafouros, M.I., Buckley, P.J., Sharp, J.A., Wang, C. (2008). The role of internationalization in explaining innovation performance. *Technovation*, 28, 63–74.

Kaplan, R.S. and Norton, D.P. (1996). *The Balanced Scorecard: Translating Strategy into Action*. Harvard Business Review Press, Boston, MA.

Katsikeas, C.S., Leonidou, L.C., Morgan, N.A. (2000). Firm-level export performance assessment: Review, evaluation, and development. *Journal of the Academy of Marketing Science*, 28, 493–511.

Kim, S.-K. and Song, O. (2009). A MAUT approach for selecting a dismantling scenario for the thermal column in KRR-1. *Annals of Nuclear Energy*, 36, 145–150.

Korab, V. and Koudelkova, P. (2016). What determines innovation in small and medium enteprises? A case study from the Czech Republic. *Transformations in Business & Economics*, 15, 78–88.

Korhonen, P., Moskowitz, H., Wallenius, J. (1992). Multiple criteria decision support – A review. *European Journal of Operational Research*, 63, 361–375.

Kotabe, M. and Czinkota, M.R. (1992). State government promotion of manufacturing exports: A gap analysis. *Journal of International Business Studies*, 23, 637–658.

Kotabe, M., Srinivasan, S.S., Aulakh, P.S. (2002). Multinationality and firm performance: The moderating role of R&D and marketing capabilities. *Journal of International Business Studies*, 33, 79–97.

Kurka, T. and Blackwood, D. (2013). Selection of MCA methods to support decision-making for renewable energy developments. *Renewable and Sustainable Energy Reviews*, 27, 225–233.

Le Moigne, J.-L. (1994). *La théorie du système général : théorie de la modélisation*. Presses Universitaires de France, Paris.

Le Moigne, J.-L. (2007). Comprendre c'est conjoindre. *Chemins de formation*, 223–231.

Le Roy, F. and Torrès, O. (2001). La place de l'innovation dans les stratégies concurrentielles des PME internationales. *Innovations*, 13, 43–60.

Lianying, Z., Jing, H., Xinxing, Z. (2012). The project management maturity model and application based on PRINCE2. *Procedia Engineering*, 29, 3691–3697.

Lileeva, A. and Trefler, D. (2010). Improved access to foreign markets raises plant-level productivity for some plants. *The Quarterly Journal of Economics*, 125, 1051–1099.

Liu, M., Li, M., Zhang, T. (2012). Empirical research on China's SMEs technology innovation engineering strategy. *Systems Engineering Procedia*, 5, 372–378.

Liu, Y., Lv, D., Ying, Y., Arndt, F., Wei, J. (2018). Improvisation for innovation: The contingent role of resource and structural factors in explaining innovation capability. *Technovation*, 74/75, 32–41.

López Rodríguez, J. and García Rodríguez, R.M. (2005). Technology and export behaviour: A resource-based view approach. *International Business Review*, 14, 539–557.

Love, J.H. and Roper, S. (2015). SME innovation, exporting and growth: A review of existing evidence. *International Small Business Journal*, 33, 28–48.

Martineau, C. and Pastoriza, D. (2016). International involvement of established SMEs: A systematic review of antecedents, outcomes and moderators. *International Business Review*, 25, 458–470.

Martínez-Román, J.A., Gamero, J., Tamayo, J.A. (2011). Analysis of innovation in SMEs using an innovative capability-based non-linear model: A study in the province of Seville (Spain). *Technovation*, 31, 459–475.

Mason, E.S. (1959). *The Corporation in Modern Society*. Harvard University Press, Cambridge, MA.

Mintzberg, H. (1979). *The Structuring of Organizations*. Pearson, Englewood Cliffs, NJ.

Moeuf, A., Pellerin, R., Lamouri, S., Tamayo-Giraldo, S., Barbaray, R. (2018). The industrial management of SMEs in the era of Industry 4.0. *International Journal of Production Research*, 56, 1118–1136.

Monreal-Pérez, J., Aragón-Sánchez, A., Sánchez-Marín, G. (2012). A longitudinal study of the relationship between export activity and innovation in the Spanish firm: The moderating role of productivity. *International Business Review*, 21, 862–877.

Montoro-Sanchez, A., Diez-Vial, I., Belso-Martinez, J.A. (2018). The evolution of the domestic network configuration as a driver of international relationships in SMEs. *International Business Review*, 27, 727–736.

Morel, L. (2007). Vers une nouvelle forme de Génie des Procédés Complexes : intégration de la capacité à innover pour l'évaluation des stratégies de développement produits-procédés. Mémoire de HdR, INPL, Nancy.

Morgan, N.A., Kaleka, A., Katsikeas, C.S. (2004). Antecedents of export venture performance: A theoretical model and empirical assessment. *Journal of Marketing*, 68, 90–108.

Morin, E. (1977). *La méthode : la nature de la nature, tome 1*. Le Seuil, Paris.

Morin, E. (1986). *La méthode : la connaissance de la connaissance, tome 3*. Le Seuil, Paris.

Morin, E. (1994). *Introduction à la pensée complexe*. ESF Éditeur, Paris.

Muller, A., Välikangas, L., Merlyn, P. (2005). Metrics for innovation: Guidelines for developing a customized suite of innovation metrics. *Strategy and Leadership*, 33, 37–45.

Navarro-García, A., Arenas-Gaitán, J., Javier Rondán-Cataluña, F., Rey-Moreno, M. (2016). Global model of export performance: Moderator role of export department. *Journal of Business Research*, 69, 1880–1886.

Nemery, P. (2009). On the use of multicriteria ranking methods in sorting problems. Thesis, Université Libre de Bruxelles, Brussels.

Nemery, P. and Lamboray, C. (2008). FlowSort: A flow-based sorting method with limiting or central profiles. *TOP 16*, 90–113.

Nieto, M.J. and Santamaría, L. (2010). Technological collaboration: Bridging the innovation gap between small and large firms. *Journal of Small Business Management*, 48, 44–69.

Noack, A. (2007). Energy models for graph clustering. *Journal of Graph Algorithms and Applications*, 11, 453–480.

Noack, A. (2009). Modularity clustering is force-directed layout. *Physical Review E*, 79, 026102.

OECD (2009). Top barriers and drivers to SME internationalisation. Working Party on SMEs and Entrepreneurship, Organisation for Economic Co-operation and Development. Report, OECD.

OECD (2018). Fostering greater SME participation in a globally integrated economy (SME Ministerial Conference, Plenary Session 3). Organisation for Economic Co-operation and Development. Report, OECD.

Okręglicka, M., Gorzeń-Mitka, I., Ogrean, C. (2015). Management challenges in the context of a complex view – SMEs perspective. *Procedia Economics and Finance, Special Issue International Scientific Conference BEM2015*, 34, 445–452.

Oliveira, J.S., Gnizy, I., Cadogan, J.W., Nizam, A. (2017). Cross-functional dispersion of export marketing decision-making and export performance: A study of UK firms, an abstract. In *Proceedings of the Academy of Marketing Science*, Rossi, P. (ed.). Springer, Cham.

Oura, M.M., Zilber, S.N., Lopes, E.L. (2015). Innovation capacity, international experience and export performance of SMEs in Brazil. *International Business Review*, 25(4), 921–932.

Pascal, B. (1976). *Pensées*. Hachette, Paris.

Penrose, E.T. (1959). *The Theory of the Growth of the Firm*. Oxford University Press, Oxford/New York.

Pettersen, N., St-Pierre, J., Brutus, S. (2011). Relation entre les compétences du dirigeant de PME et la performance de son entreprise. Apport d'un instrument de mesure multisource. *Revue internationale PME*, 24.

Pierre, A. and Fernandez, A.-S. (2018). Going deeper into SMEs' innovation capacity: An empirical exploration of innovation capacity factors. *Journal of Innovation Economics*, 25, 139–181.

Pla-Barber, J. and Alegre, J. (2007). Analysing the link between export intensity, innovation and firm size in a science-based industry. *International Business Review*, 16, 275–293.

Porter, M.E. (1998). *Competitive Strategy: Techniques for Analyzing Industries and Competitors*. Free Press, New York.

Potier, O., Brun, J., Le Masson, P., Weil, B. (2015). How innovative design can contribute to chemical and process engineering development? Opening new innovation paths by applying the C–K method. *Chemical Engineering Research and Design*, 103, 108–122.

Raymond, L. and St-Pierre, J. (2013). Strategic capability configurations for the internationalization of SMEs: A study in equifinality. *International Small Business Journal*, 31, 82–102.

Ribau, C.P., Moreira, A.C., Raposo, M. (2019). The role of exploitative and exploratory innovation in export performance: An analysis of plastics industry SMEs. *European Journal of International Management*, 13, 224–246.

Rodrigues, J.F., Traina, A.J.M., de Oliveira, M.C.F., Traina, A.J.M. (2006). Reviewing data visualization: An analytical taxonomical study. *10th International Conference on Information Visualization*, 713–720.

Rodriguez, R.P. and Hechanova, M.R.M. (2014). A study of culture dimensions, organizational ambidexterity, and perceived innovation in teams. *Journal of Technology Management & Innovation*, 9, 21–33.

Roper, S. and Love, J.H. (2002). Innovation and export performance: Evidence from the UK and German manufacturing plants. *Research Policy*, 31, 1087–1102.

Saaty, T.L. (1980). *The Analytic Hierarchy Process: Planning, Priority Setting, Resource Allocation*. McGraw-Hill, New York.

Saaty, T.L. and Kearns, K.P. (1985). *Analytical Planning: The Organization of Systems*. Pergamon Press, Oxford/New York.

Sanayei, A., Farid Mousavi, S., Abdi, M.R., Mohaghar, A. (2008). An integrated group decision-making process for supplier selection and order allocation using multi-attribute utility theory and linear programming. *Journal of the Franklin Institute*, 345, 731–747.

Sauner-Leroy, J.-B. (2000). Nature de l'environnement, style de direction et performance des firmes : un test de la théorie de la contingence. *Perspectives en Management stratégique, 9ème conférence internationale de management stratégique*, Montpellier.

Schmitt, C., Julien, P.-A., Lachance, R. (2002). Pour une lecture des problèmes complexes en PME : approche conceptuelle et expérimentation. *Revue internationale PME*, 15, 35–62.

Schumpeter, J.A. (1934). The theory of economic development. *Harvard Economic Studies*, 46.

Seens, D. (2015). SME profile: Canadian exporters. Report from industry Canada, small business branch, research and analysis directorate [Online]. Available at: https://www.ic.gc.ca/eic/site/061.nsf/eng/h_02925.html.

Sepulveda, J., Gonzalez, J., Camargo, M., Alfaro, M. (2010). A metrics-based diagnosis tool for enhancing innovation capabilities in SMEs. *International Journal of Computers*, 5, 919–928.

Seringhaus, F.H.R. and Rosson, P.J. (1990). *Government Export Promotion: A Global Perspective*. Routledge, London.

St-Pierre, J. and Cadieux, L. (2012). La conception de la performance : quels liens avec le profil entrepreneurial des propriétaires dirigeants de PME ? *Revue de l'entrepreneuriat*, 10, 33–52.

St-Pierre, J., Raymond, L., Laurin, F., Uwizeyemungu, S. (2011). Mondialisation et internationalisation des PME : le comportement des PME manufacturières québécoises. CIRANO research report, Institut de recherche sur les PME, Université du Québec à Trois-Rivières, Trois-Rivières.

Szczepanski, M. (2016). Barriers to SME growth in Europe. Working paper PE 583, 788, European Parliamentary Research Service.

Taneja, S., Pryor, M.G., Hayek, M. (2016). Leaping innovation barriers to small business longevity. *Journal of Business Strategy*, 37(3), 44–51.

Teece, D.J., Pisano, G., Shuen, A. (1997). Dynamic capabilities and strategic management. *Strategic Management Journal*, 18, 509–533.

Terziovski, M. (2010). Innovation practice and its performance implications in small and medium enterprises (SMEs) in the manufacturing sector: A resource-based view. *Strategic Management Journal*, 31(8), 892–902.

Thomä, J. and Bizer, K. (2013). To protect or not to protect? Modes of appropriability in the small enterprise sector. *Research Policy*, 42, 35–49.

Thornhill, S. (2006). Knowledge, innovation and firm performance in high and low technology regimes. *Journal of Business Venturing*, 21, 687–703.

Tidd, J. and Thuriaux-Alemán, B. (2016). Innovation management practices: Cross-sectorial adoption, variation, and effectiveness. *R&D Management*, 46, 1024–1043.

Tirole, J. (1988). *The Theory of Industrial Organization*. MIT Press, Cambridge, MA.

Torrès, O. (2015). Petitesse des entreprises et grossissement des effets de proximité. *Revue française de gestion*, 41, 333–352.

Torrès, O. and Julien, P.-A. (2005). Specificity and denaturing of small business. *International Small Business Journal*, 23, 355–377.

Urbinati, A., Chiaroni, D., Chiesa, V., Franzò, S., Frattini, F. (2018). An exploratory analysis on the contextual factors that influence disruptive innovation: The case of Uber. *International Journal of Innovation and Technology Management*, 15(3), 1850024.

Uzunidis, D. (2016). Propaedeutics in the theory of the industrial organisation: The SCP (structure, conduct, performance) model. *Journal of Innovation Economics & Management*, 20(2), 197–215.

Wendler, R. (2012). The maturity of maturity model research: A systematic mapping study. *Information and Software Technology*, 54, 1317–1339.

WTO (2016). World trade report 2016: Levelling the trading field for SMEs. Report, World Trade Organization.

Yam, R.C.M., Guan, J.C., Pun, K.F., Tang, E.P.Y. (2004). An audit of technological innovation capabilities in Chinese firms: Some empirical findings in Beijing, China. *Research Policy*, 33, 1123–1140.

Yatchinovsky, A. (2012). *L'approche systémique : pour gérer l'incertitude et la complexité*, 5ème édition. ESF Editeur, Issy-les-Moulineaux.

Yau, N. (2012). *Visualize This!* Wiley-VCH, Weinheim.

Yin, R.K. (2013). *Case Study Research: Design and Methods*. SAGE Publications, Thousand Oaks, CA.

Zawislak, P.A., Alves, A.C., Tello-Gamarra, J., Barbieux, D., Reichert, F.M. (2014). Innovation capability: From technology development to transaction capability. *Journal of Technology Management and Innovation*, 7, 14–25.

Zehir, C., Köle, M., Yıldız, H. (2015). The mediating role of innovation capability on market orientation and export performance: An implementation on SMEs in Turkey. *Social and Behavioral Sciences*, 207, 700–708.

Zeng, S.X., Xie, X.M., Tam, C.M. (2010). Relationship between cooperation networks and innovation performance of SMEs. *Technovation*, 30, 181–194.

Zopounidis, C. and Doumpos, M. (2002). Multicriteria classification and sorting methods: A literature review. *European Journal of Operational Research*, 138, 229–246.

Index

Other titles from

iSTE

in

Innovation, Entrepreneurship and Management

2021

ARCADE Jacques
Strategic Engineering (Innovation and Technology Set – Volume 11)

BÉRANGER Jérôme, RIZOULIÈRES Roland
The Digital Revolution in Health (Health and Innovation Set – Volume 2)

BOBILLIER CHAUMON Marc-Eric
Digital Transformations in the Challenge of Activity and Work: Understanding and Supporting Technological Changes (Technological Changes and Human Resources Set – Volume 3)

BUCLET Nicolas
Territorial Ecology and Socio-ecological Transition (Smart Innovation Set – Volume 34)

DIMOTIKALIS Yannis, KARAGRIGORIOU Alex, PARPOULA Christina, SKIADIS Christos H
Applied Modeling Techniques and Data Analysis 1: Computational Data Analysis Methods and Tools (Big Data, Artificial Intelligence and Data Analysis Set - Volume 7)
Applied Modeling Techniques and Data Analysis 2: Financial, Demographic, Stochastic and Statistical Models and Methods (Big Data, Artificial Intelligence and Data Analysis Set – Volume 8)

DISPAS Christophe, KAYANAKIS Georges, SERVEL Nicolas, STRIUKOVA Ludmila
Innovation and Financial Markets
(Innovation between Risk and Reward Set – Volume 7)

GOGLIN Christian
Emotions and Values in Equity Crowdfunding Investment Choices 2: Modeling and Empirical Study

GRENIER Corinne, OIRY Ewan
Altering Frontiers: Organizational Innovations in Healthcare (Health and Innovation Set – Volume 1)

GUERRIER Claudine
Security and Its Challenges in the 21st Century (Innovation and Technology Set – Volume 12)

HELLER David
Performance of Valuation Methods in Financial Transactions (Modern Finance, Management Innovation and Economic Growth Set – Volume 4)

LEHMANN Paul-Jacques
Liberalism and Capitalism Today

UZUNIDIS Dimitri, KASMI Fedoua, ADATTO Laurent
Innovation Economics, Engineering and Management Handbook 1: Main Themes
Innovation Economics, Engineering and Management Handbook 2: Special Themes

2020

ACH Yves-Alain, RMADI-SAÏD Sandra
Financial Information and Brand Value: Reflections, Challenges and Limitations

ANDREOSSO-O'CALLAGHAN Bernadette, DZEVER Sam, JAUSSAUD Jacques, TAYLOR Robert
Sustainable Development and Energy Transition in Europe and Asia
(Innovation and Technology Set – Volume 9)

BEN SLIMANE Sonia, M'HENNI Hatem
Entrepreneurship and Development: Realities and Future Prospects
(Smart Innovation Set – Volume 30)

CHOUTEAU Marianne, FOREST Joëlle, NGUYEN Céline
Innovation for Society: The P.S.I. Approach
(Smart Innovation Set – Volume 28)

CORON Clotilde
Quantifying Human Resources: Uses and Analysis
(Technological Changes and Human Resources Set – Volume 2)

CORON Clotilde, GILBERT Patrick
Technological Change
(Technological Changes and Human Resources Set – Volume 1)

CERDIN Jean-Luc, PERETTI Jean-Marie
The Success of Apprenticeships: Views of Stakeholders on Training and Learning (Human Resources Management Set – Volume 3)

DELCHET-COCHET Karen
Circular Economy: From Waste Reduction to Value Creation
(Economic Growth Set – Volume 2)

DIDAY Edwin, GUAN Rong, SAPORTA Gilbert, WANG Huiwen
Advances in Data Science
(Big Data, Artificial Intelligence and Data Analysis Set – Volume 4)

DOS SANTOS PAULINO Victor
Innovation Trends in the Space Industry
(Smart Innovation Set – Volume 25)

GASMI Nacer
Corporate Innovation Strategies: Corporate Social Responsibility and Shared Value Creation
(Smart Innovation Set – Volume 33)

GOGLIN Christian
Emotions and Values in Equity Crowdfunding Investment Choices 1: Transdisciplinary Theoretical Approach

GUILHON Bernard
Venture Capital and the Financing of Innovation
(Innovation Between Risk and Reward Set – Volume 6)

LATOUCHE Pascal
Open Innovation: Human Set-up
(Innovation and Technology Set – Volume 10)

LIMA Marcos
Entrepreneurship and Innovation Education: Frameworks and Tools
(Smart Innovation Set – Volume 32)

MACHADO Carolina, DAVIM J. Paulo
Sustainable Management for Managers and Engineers

MAKRIDES Andreas, KARAGRIGORIOU Alex, SKIADAS Christos H.
Data Analysis and Applications 3: Computational, Classification, Financial, Statistical and Stochastic Methods
(Big Data, Artificial Intelligence and Data Analysis Set – Volume 5)
Data Analysis and Applications 4: Financial Data Analysis and Methods
(Big Data, Artificial Intelligence and Data Analysis Set – Volume 6)

MASSOTTE Pierre, CORSI Patrick
Complex Decision-Making in Economy and Finance

MEUNIER François-Xavier
Dual Innovation Systems: Concepts, Tools and Methods
(Smart Innovation Set – Volume 31)

MICHAUD Thomas
Science Fiction and Innovation Design (Innovation in Engineering and Technology Set – Volume 6)

MONINO Jean-Louis
Data Control: Major Challenge for the Digital Society (Smart Innovation Set – Volume 29)

MORLAT Clément
Sustainable Productive System: Eco-development versus Sustainable Development (Smart Innovation Set – Volume 26)

SAULAIS Pierre, ERMINE Jean-Louis
Knowledge Management in Innovative Companies 2: Understanding and Deploying a KM Plan within a Learning Organization (Smart Innovation Set – Volume 27)

2019

AMENDOLA Mario, GAFFARD Jean-Luc
Disorder and Public Concern Around Globalization

BARBAROUX Pierre
Disruptive Technology and Defence Innovation Ecosystems (Innovation in Engineering and Technology Set – Volume 5)

DOU Henri, JUILLET Alain, CLERC Philippe
Strategic Intelligence for the Future 1: A New Strategic and Operational Approach
Strategic Intelligence for the Future 2: A New Information Function Approach

FRIKHA Azza
Measurement in Marketing: Operationalization of Latent Constructs

FRIMOUSSE Soufyane
Innovation and Agility in the Digital Age (Human Resources Management Set – Volume 2)

GAY Claudine, SZOSTAK Bérangère L.
Innovation and Creativity in SMEs: Challenges, Evolutions and Prospects (Smart Innovation Set – Volume 21)

GORIA Stéphane, HUMBERT Pierre, ROUSSEL Benoît
Information, Knowledge and Agile Creativity (Smart Innovation Set – Volume 22)

HELLER David
Investment Decision-making Using Optional Models (Economic Growth Set – Volume 2)

HELLER David, DE CHADIRAC Sylvain, HALAOUI Lana, JOUVET Camille
The Emergence of Start-ups (Economic Growth Set – Volume 1)

HÉRAUD Jean-Alain, KERR Fiona, BURGER-HELMCHEN Thierry
Creative Management of Complex Systems (Smart Innovation Set – Volume 19)

LATOUCHE Pascal
Open Innovation: Corporate Incubator (Innovation and Technology Set – Volume 7)

LEHMANN Paul-Jacques
The Future of the Euro Currency

LEIGNEL Jean-Louis, MÉNAGER Emmanuel, YABLONSKY Serge
Sustainable Enterprise Performance: A Comprehensive Evaluation Method

LIÈVRE Pascal, AUBRY Monique, GAREL Gilles
Management of Extreme Situations: From Polar Expeditions to Exploration-Oriented Organizations

MILLOT Michel
Embarrassment of Product Choices 2: Towards a Society of Well-being

N'GOALA Gilles, PEZ-PÉRARD Virginie, PRIM-ALLAZ Isabelle
Augmented Customer Strategy: CRM in the Digital Age

NIKOLOVA Blagovesta
The RRI Challenge: Responsibilization in a State of Tension with Market Regulation
(Innovation and Responsibility Set – Volume 3)

PELLEGRIN-BOUCHER Estelle, ROY Pierre
Innovation in the Cultural and Creative Industries
(Innovation and Technology Set – Volume 8)

PRIOLON Joël
Financial Markets for Commodities

QUINIOU Matthieu
Blockchain: The Advent of Disintermediation

RAVIX Joël-Thomas, DESCHAMPS Marc
Innovation and Industrial Policies
(Innovation between Risk and Reward Set – Volume 5)

ROGER Alain, VINOT Didier
Skills Management: New Applications, New Questions
(Human Resources Management Set – Volume 1)

SAULAIS Pierre, ERMINE Jean-Louis
Knowledge Management in Innovative Companies 1: Understanding and Deploying a KM Plan within a Learning Organization
(Smart Innovation Set – Volume 23)

SERVAJEAN-HILST Romaric
Co-innovation Dynamics: The Management of Client-Supplier Interactions for Open Innovation
(Smart Innovation Set – Volume 20)

SKIADAS Christos H., BOZEMAN James R.
Data Analysis and Applications 1: Clustering and Regression, Modeling-estimating, Forecasting and Data Mining
(Big Data, Artificial Intelligence and Data Analysis Set – Volume 2)
Data Analysis and Applications 2: Utilization of Results in Europe and Other Topics
(Big Data, Artificial Intelligence and Data Analysis Set – Volume 3)

UZUNIDIS Dimitri
Systemic Innovation: Entrepreneurial Strategies and Market Dynamics

VIGEZZI Michel
World Industrialization: Shared Inventions, Competitive Innovations and Social Dynamics
(Smart Innovation Set – Volume 24)

2018

BURKHARDT Kirsten
Private Equity Firms: Their Role in the Formation of Strategic Alliances

CALLENS Stéphane
Creative Globalization
(Smart Innovation Set – Volume 16)

CASADELLA Vanessa
Innovation Systems in Emerging Economies: MINT – Mexico, Indonesia, Nigeria, Turkey
(Smart Innovation Set – Volume 18)

CHOUTEAU Marianne, FOREST Joëlle, NGUYEN Céline
Science, Technology and Innovation Culture
(Innovation in Engineering and Technology Set – Volume 3)

CORLOSQUET-HABART Marine, JANSSEN Jacques
Big Data for Insurance Companies
(Big Data, Artificial Intelligence and Data Analysis Set – Volume 1)

CROS Françoise
Innovation and Society
(Smart Innovation Set – Volume 15)

DEBREF Romain
Environmental Innovation and Ecodesign: Certainties and Controversies
(Smart Innovation Set – Volume 17)

DOMINGUEZ Noémie
SME Internationalization Strategies: Innovation to Conquer New Markets

ERMINE Jean-Louis
Knowledge Management: The Creative Loop
(Innovation and Technology Set – Volume 5)

GILBERT Patrick, BOBADILLA Natalia, GASTALDI Lise,
LE BOULAIRE Martine, LELEBINA Olga
Innovation, Research and Development Management

IBRAHIMI Mohammed
Mergers & Acquisitions: Theory, Strategy, Finance

LEMAÎTRE Denis
Training Engineers for Innovation

LÉVY Aldo, BEN BOUHENI Faten, AMMI Chantal
Financial Management: USGAAP and IFRS Standards
(Innovation and Technology Set – Volume 6)

MILLOT Michel
Embarrassment of Product Choices 1: How to Consume Differently

PANSERA Mario, OWEN Richard
Innovation and Development: The Politics at the Bottom of the Pyramid
(Innovation and Responsibility Set – Volume 2)

RICHEZ Yves
Corporate Talent Detection and Development

SACHETTI Philippe, ZUPPINGER Thibaud
New Technologies and Branding
(Innovation and Technology Set – Volume 4)

SAMIER Henri
Intuition, Creativity, Innovation

TEMPLE Ludovic, COMPAORÉ SAWADOGO Eveline M.F.W.
Innovation Processes in Agro-Ecological Transitions in Developing Countries
(Innovation in Engineering and Technology Set – Volume 2)

UZUNIDIS Dimitri
Collective Innovation Processes: Principles and Practices
(Innovation in Engineering and Technology Set – Volume 4)

VAN HOOREBEKE Delphine
The Management of Living Beings or Emo-management

2017

AÏT-EL-HADJ Smaïl
The Ongoing Technological System
(Smart Innovation Set – Volume 11)

BAUDRY Marc, DUMONT Béatrice
Patents: Prompting or Restricting Innovation?
(Smart Innovation Set – Volume 12)

BÉRARD Céline, TEYSSIER Christine
Risk Management: Lever for SME Development and Stakeholder Value Creation

CHALENÇON Ludivine
Location Strategies and Value Creation of International Mergers and Acquisitions

CHAUVEL Danièle, BORZILLO Stefano
The Innovative Company: An Ill-defined Object
(Innovation between Risk and Reward Set – Volume 1)

CORSI Patrick
Going Past Limits To Growth

D'ANDRIA Aude, GABARRET Inés
Building 21st Century Entrepreneurship
(Innovation and Technology Set – Volume 2)

DAIDJ Nabyla
Cooperation, Coopetition and Innovation
(Innovation and Technology Set – Volume 3)

FERNEZ-WALCH Sandrine
The Multiple Facets of Innovation Project Management
(Innovation between Risk and Reward Set – Volume 4)

FOREST Joëlle
Creative Rationality and Innovation
(Smart Innovation Set – Volume 14)

GUILHON Bernard
Innovation and Production Ecosystems
(Innovation between Risk and Reward Set – Volume 2)

HAMMOUDI Abdelhakim, DAIDJ Nabyla
Game Theory Approach to Managerial Strategies and Value Creation
(Diverse and Global Perspectives on Value Creation Set – Volume 3)

LALLEMENT Rémi
Intellectual Property and Innovation Protection: New Practices and New Policy Issues
(Innovation between Risk and Reward Set – Volume 3)

LAPERCHE Blandine
Enterprise Knowledge Capital
(Smart Innovation Set – Volume 13)

LEBERT Didier, EL YOUNSI Hafida
International Specialization Dynamics
(Smart Innovation Set – Volume 9)

MAESSCHALCK Marc
Reflexive Governance for Research and Innovative Knowledge
(Responsible Research and Innovation Set – Volume 6)

MASSOTTE Pierre
Ethics in Social Networking and Business 1: Theory, Practice and Current Recommendations
Ethics in Social Networking and Business 2: The Future and Changing Paradigms

MASSOTTE Pierre, CORSI Patrick
Smart Decisions in Complex Systems

MEDINA Mercedes, HERRERO Mónica, URGELLÉS Alicia
Current and Emerging Issues in the Audiovisual Industry
(Diverse and Global Perspectives on Value Creation Set – Volume 1)

MICHAUD Thomas
Innovation, Between Science and Science Fiction
(Smart Innovation Set – Volume 10)

PELLÉ Sophie
Business, Innovation and Responsibility
(Responsible Research and Innovation Set – Volume 7)

SAVIGNAC Emmanuelle
The Gamification of Work: The Use of Games in the Workplace

SUGAHARA Satoshi, DAIDJ Nabyla, USHIO Sumitaka
Value Creation in Management Accounting and Strategic Management: An Integrated Approach
(Diverse and Global Perspectives on Value Creation Set –Volume 2)

UZUNIDIS Dimitri, SAULAIS Pierre
Innovation Engines: Entrepreneurs and Enterprises in a Turbulent World
(Innovation in Engineering and Technology Set – Volume 1)

2016

BARBAROUX Pierre, ATTOUR Amel, SCHENK Eric
Knowledge Management and Innovation
(Smart Innovation Set – Volume 6)

BEN BOUHENI Faten, AMMI Chantal, LEVY Aldo
Banking Governance, Performance And Risk-Taking: Conventional Banks Vs Islamic Banks

BOUTILLIER Sophie, CARRÉ Denis, LEVRATTO Nadine
Entrepreneurial Ecosystems (Smart Innovation Set – Volume 2)

BOUTILLIER Sophie, UZUNIDIS Dimitri
The Entrepreneur (Smart Innovation Set – Volume 8)

BOUVARD Patricia, SUZANNE Hervé
Collective Intelligence Development in Business

GALLAUD Delphine, LAPERCHE Blandine
Circular Economy, Industrial Ecology and Short Supply Chains
(Smart Innovation Set – Volume 4)

GUERRIER Claudine
Security and Privacy in the Digital Era
(Innovation and Technology Set – Volume 1)

MEGHOUAR Hicham
Corporate Takeover Targets

MONINO Jean-Louis, SEDKAOUI Soraya
Big Data, Open Data and Data Development
(Smart Innovation Set – Volume 3)

MOREL Laure, LE ROUX Serge
Fab Labs: Innovative User
(Smart Innovation Set – Volume 5)

PICARD Fabienne, TANGUY Corinne
Innovations and Techno-ecological Transition
(Smart Innovation Set – Volume 7)

2015

CASADELLA Vanessa, LIU Zeting, DIMITRI Uzunidis
Innovation Capabilities and Economic Development in Open Economies
(Smart Innovation Set – Volume 1)

CORSI Patrick, MORIN Dominique
Sequencing Apple's DNA

CORSI Patrick, NEAU Erwan
Innovation Capability Maturity Model

FAIVRE-TAVIGNOT Bénédicte
Social Business and Base of the Pyramid

GODÉ Cécile
Team Coordination in Extreme Environments

MAILLARD Pierre
Competitive Quality and Innovation

MASSOTTE Pierre, CORSI Patrick
Operationalizing Sustainability

MASSOTTE Pierre, CORSI Patrick
Sustainability Calling

2014

DUBÉ Jean, LEGROS Diègo
Spatial Econometrics Using Microdata

LESCA Humbert, LESCA Nicolas
Strategic Decisions and Weak Signals

2013

HABART-CORLOSQUET Marine, JANSSEN Jacques, MANCA Raimondo
VaR Methodology for Non-Gaussian Finance

2012

DAL PONT Jean-Pierre
Process Engineering and Industrial Management

MAILLARD Pierre
Competitive Quality Strategies

POMEROL Jean-Charles
Decision-Making and Action

SZYLAR Christian
UCITS Handbook